C for Programmers

WILEY SERIES IN COMPUTING

Consulting Editor
Professor D. W. Barron
Department of Computer Studies, University of Southampton,
UK

C for Programmers

L. Ammeraal

Christelijke Hogere Technische School
Hilversum, The Netherlands

JOHN WILEY & SONS
Chichester · New York · Brisbane · Toronto · Singapore

Copyright © 1986 by John Wiley & Sons Ltd.

Library of Congress Cataloging-in-Publication Data:

Ammeraal, Leendert.
  C for programmers.

  Bibliography: p.
  Includes index.
  1. C (Computer program language)   I. Title.
QA76.73.C15A46   1986   005.13'3   86-9154
ISBN 0 471 91128 3

British Library Cataloguing in Publication Data:

Ammeraal, Leendert
  C for programmers
  1. C (Computer program language)
  I. Title
  005.13'3   QA76.73.C15

ISBN 0 471 91128 3

Printed and bound in Great Britain by The Universities Press (Belfast) Ltd.

Contents

Preface

This book is intended for those who want to learn the C programming language efficiently. I have tried to be complete with respect to the language in fewer pages than most competitive books, omitting general issues which the reader is probably already familiar with, or, if not, he can either learn from other sources or invent himself. For example, I explain neither the binary representation of numbers nor any 'program-development method' (whatever that may be). Many examples in this book are complete programs of moderate size. Most of these are useful only to illustrate the subjects under discussion, not to be executed in real applications. In other words, they are subordinate to the explanation of the C language. Still, there are a few programs which are instructive not only in learning C but also with respect to real applications. An example is an elegant and efficient sorting method for files, known as natural merge sort. It is dealt with in Chapter 6, along with a program for binary file search, which demonstrates how we can update a file with direct access. For reasons of consistency and portability, all file handling in this book is on the level technically known as 'standard I/O'. A reasonable number of widely available library functions are included, but I do not attempt to render the reference manual for the reader's particular system superfluous. I aim rather at the opposite: to interest him so much that after studying this introduction he will not only enjoy programming in C but also be prepared to consult more authoritative books on C and on programming in general.

L. Ammeraal

CHAPTER 1

Introduction

The C programming language was designed and implemented by D. M. Ritchie of Bell Laboratories. Though sometimes regarded as a language for systems programming, C can be used very well for a great variety of applications.

Like advanced textbooks on mathematics, for the uninitiated, C programs are sometimes hard to read. Unlike mathematics, programming is often underestimated with respect to its difficulties. It is a mistake to ascribe these difficulties to concise notations and to think that more verbose language constructions than those offered by C should be helpful. On the contrary, brief notations that are understood only by experts are of great value in all exact sciences, including computer science. C constructs that are considered too 'cryptic' by outsiders are usually highly appreciated by the users of this language.

The C language is also well known for the freedom it offers to the user. Obviously, this freedom can be misused, but many professional programmers need it, and use it wisely. As a consequence of this freedom, inaccurate users of C will soon discover that it is extremely easy to write programs that perform actions different from what was intended. In contrast to other languages, and to the astonishment of the inexperienced user, those programs often turn out to be syntactically correct. The compiler will therefore not complain, and a very technical run-time error message, an infinite loop or a wrong result will ensue. For example, if by mistake we write a single equal sign (=) in a position where two of these characters (==) belong, it may be very hard to find out why we obtain wrong results. This is not a serious disadvantage of the language. In programming we have to be careful anyhow, and it is only reasonable that wrong instructions should lead to wrong results.

The qualities of a programming language are better explained by concrete examples than by abstract discussions. We shall begin with a simple program which does not immediately illustrate the above remarks.

Suppose that we are interested in the smallest integer n that satisfies the following inequality:

$$1 + \frac{1}{2} + \frac{1}{3} + \ldots + \frac{1}{n} \geq 5$$

The following C program computes and prints that value.

```
/* NVALUE: Compute the smallest n satisfying
                1 + 1/2 + 1/3 + . . . + 1/n >= 5              */
main( )
{ int n = 0; double s = 0.0;
   while (s < 5.0)
   { n = n + 1;
     s = s + 1.0/n;
   }
   printf ("%d\n", n);
}
```

In this introduction we shall only briefly explain this program. The language elements used will be discussed more systematically later in the book. The first two lines contain comment for the human reader: from the character pair /* the compiler will simply skip everything up to and including the first character pair */ that follows. (The term 'compiler' is used for the program that translates our C program to some internal code.) We shall use the name *NVALUE,* occurring in this comment, if we want to refer to the program later.

Every C program contains one or more functions, each of the form

```
. . . f( . . . ) . . .
   { . . .
   }
```

where f stands for the name of the function (three dots . . . denoting optional program text). One of these functions must have the name *main,* and program-execution will start at the beginning of that function. Functions may or may not have parameters, written between parentheses after the function name. The parentheses must be present even if there are no parameters. This explains the third line of program *NVALUE.* We distinguish several data types. Here we have the types *int* and *double,* the former being used for integers and the latter for double-precision floating point. Values of type int are exact but rather limited, depending on the hardware. On many machines these values must be less than 2^{15} or 2^{31}. Floating-point types allow much larger values and are not restricted to whole numbers. However, floating-point values are only represented in a finite precision. In program *NVALUE* we have declared n to be of type int and s of type double. In their declarations variables can be given initial values, or, in other words, they can be initialized. Here both n and s are initialized to zero.

A program fragment of the form

```
while ( . . . )
   { . . .
   } . . .
```

is called a *while-statement.* In the while-statement in program *NVALUE* the value of variable s is repeatedly compared with 5. Each time that s is less than 5, n is incremented by one and s is increased by $1/n$. As soon as s has at least the value 5, the value of n is printed and the program halts. It turns out that this value of n is 83. Traditionally we say that something is *printed,* even if it is only displayed on the screen of our terminal, which is more customary nowadays. The letter f in the function name *printf* stands for 'formatted'. We not only tell *what* is to be printed but also *how* it is to be done. In our example the format string *"%d\n"* contains the format item *%d* and the newline character \n. According to *%d*, the value of n is printed in a decimal representation in just as many positions as are needed. This is followed by a transition to the beginning of a new line as a result of the occurrence of \n in the format string. A more interesting example is:

    printf("Result:\n n = %3d   s = %9.7f\n", n, s);

If we use this line in program *NVALUE* instead of the old line with *printf* we will have the following output:

    Result:
      $n =$ 83 $s = 5.0020683$

The format string contains the format items *%3d* and *%9.7f*. This causes n and s to be printed in three and nine positions, respectively. The 7 in 9.7 says that we want seven digits after the period. All other characters in the format string are printed literally. Notice the effect of the newline characters and the blanks that occur in the format string.

EXERCISES

1.1   What word and what number will be printed by the following program?

```
main( )
{ printf("To"); printf("get"); printf("her");
  printf("%7.1f", 54321.1492); printf("%4d\n", 2345);
}
```

1.2   Estimate the value of s printed by:

```
main( )
{ int n = 1; double s = 0.0;
  while (n < 10000)
  { s = s + 1.0/n;
    n = n + n;
  }
  printf("The sum is %6.3f\n", s);
}
```

CHAPTER 2

Simple expressions and some statements

This chapter deals with a number of elementary concepts. Its contents will enable the reader to write a class of simple but useful programs, and prepare him to study the more advanced topics in the rest of the book, some of which are closely related to the subjects discussed here.

2.1 IDENTIFIERS AND KEYWORDS

Names of variables and of some other program elements are called identifiers. They are composed of

letters:	$a, \ldots, z, \quad A, \ldots, Z$
digits:	$0, 1, \ldots, 9$
the underscore:	_

but they must not begin with a digit. Capital and small letters are distinct, so there are 52 letters. Examples of identifiers are:

largest_number
a
A
H2SO4

Note that the second and the third identifier, *a* and *A*, are distinct. For some compilers, only the first *n* characters of an identifier are significant, where *n* is some fixed value, defined in the reference manual of the compiler.

We must not choose the following identifiers, since they are reserved for use as keywords:

auto, break, case, char, continue, default, do, double, else, extern, float, for, goto, if, int, long, register, return, short, sizeof, static, struct, switch, typedef, union, unsigned, void, while

Some compilers also regard *asm* and *fortran* as keywords.

2.2 CONSTANTS

Integer constants can be written in various notations. As usual, a sequence of digits (not beginning with 0) is interpreted as a decimal representation of an integer number. If the first digit is 0 we have an octal representation, so then the digits 8 and 9 are not allowed. For example, 027 and 23 are different notations for the same number, since $2 \times 8 + 7 = 23$. We can also use hexadecimal representations, which begin with 0X or 0x. The hexadecimal digits A, B, C, D, E, F (or a, b, c, d, e, f)

have the values 10, 11, 12, 13, 14, 15, respectively. For example, $0XF3$ has the value $15 \times 16 + 3 = 243$. All constants are of some type. Integer constants normally have type *int*. However, they have type *long int* (or, briefly, *long*) either if they are too large for type int or if they are immediately followed by the letter L (or l). Thus $12L$ has type long, and so has 123456789, if the latter constant is too large for int (and not too large for long int).

Floating-point constants always have type *double*. These constants contain a decimal point or the letter E (or e). Examples are:

456.789
.123
1.
$18E-3$
$.65e12$
$3.e8$

The notations $18E-3$, $18e-3$ and 0.018 denote the same real number.

One character surrounded by single quotes denotes a character constant. Here are some examples:

$'A'$
$'a'$
$' '$
$'?'$

We use the backslash \ to denote non-graphic characters and other special characters that would otherwise cause problems:

$'\n'$	newline (linefeed)
$'\t'$	horizontal tab
$'\b'$	backspace
$'\r'$	carriage return
$'\f'$	form feed
$'\\'$	backslash
$'\''$	single quote

We can also use the form

$'\ddd'$

where the backslash is followed by, at most, three octal digits specifying the desired internal value of the character. An important special case of this is the null character $'\0'$, to be distinguished from $'0'$.

A sequence of characters surrounded by double quotes is a string constant. Again the backslash can be used for special characters which otherwise would cause problems. They include the double quote, which in a string is written as two characters \". Examples of string constants are:

$"ABC"$
$"A"$
$"%d\n\n"$
$"A\"BC\\D"$

The last example denotes the following sequence of six characters:

   A"BC\D

Internally, a null character is added immediately after the final character of a string. For example, the string constant *"ABC"* is internally stored in four bytes, the fourth byte containing the character *'\0'*. A string constant containing only one character, such as *"A"*, should not be confused with the corresponding character constant (*'A'*).

The string *"ABC\nDEF"* should be regarded as a two-line string, so a string constant of one line, when printed, can produce several lines in the output. We can also achieve the opposite of this, writing a string constant on two or more lines, although it is conceptually a one-line string. We then write a backslash at the very end of the lines that are to be continued. Thus the statement

   *printf("PQR\
   STU");*

prints the string

   PQRSTU

provided that the *S* of *STU* is in the first position of the program line.

2.3 ARITHMETIC OPERATIONS

The operators $+$, $-$, $*$, used in the assignment statement

   $x = a - (b - c * d) + e;$

have the effect we expect. It goes without saying that multiplication ($*$) has higher precedence than addition ($+$) or subtraction ($-$).

The operator $/$ for division deserves our special attention. There are in fact two distinct division operations, and the slash ($/$) is used for both. If we divide an integer by another integer, we obtain an integer result:

   $39 / 5 = 7$

If in the division x/y at least one of the operands x and y has floating-point type, the result has floating-point type. Incidentally, this also applies to addition, subtraction and multiplication. For the latter three operations the value of the result is normally not seriously affected by the type of the operands. For example:

   $4 \ + 3 = 7$ (integer)
   $4.0 + 3 = 7.0$ (floating point)

With $/$, however, the data types of the operands normally have a drastic influence on the result:

   $4 \ / 3 = 1$ (integer)
   $4.0 / 3 = 1.333\ldots$ (floating point)

Here not only the types of the results but also their values differ! The following example shows the four possibilities for the operand types:

```
39  /5  = 7
39.0/5  = 7.8
39  /5.0 = 7.8
39.0/5.0 = 7.8
```

The division result obtained by the / operator is called the *quotient.* Integer division has another interesting result, namely the *remainder,* obtained by the operator %. For example, 39 % 5 gives 4, since $39 = 7 \times 5 + 4$.

Expressions contain variables, constants, operators and parentheses. Example of expressions are:

length
123
$b + 246.8 * c$
$a * (b - c) / d$
$(-b + D) / (2 * a)$

In the last example, the minus sign is a so-called *unary* operator, to be distinguished from the binary operator $-$ in $(b - c)$. There is no unary plus operator in C.

2.4 COMPARISON AND LOGICAL OPERATORS

For decisions and repetitions we need the following operators:

C notation	Meaning
<	less than
>	greater than
<=	less than or equal to
>=	greater than or equal to
==	equal to
!=	not equal to
&&	logical and
||	logical or
!	not

In technical terms,

$$< \quad > \quad <= \quad >=$$

are relational operators, and

$$== \quad !=$$

are equality operators.

In C the expression $a < b$ is of integer type. Its value is either 0, denoting false, or 1, denoting true. Thus

$$100 + (30 < 40)$$

is a valid expression, and its value is 101. In contexts that we intuitively consider logical not only 1 but also other non-zero values are interpreted as true. Therefore

if $(n \mathrel{!=} 0) \ldots$

can be replaced with

if $(n) \ldots$

The logical operators && (and) and || (or) have a very attractive characteristic. It is guaranteed that their second operand will not be evaluated if this is not needed to determine the result. Since false and true are coded by 0 and 1, respectively,

    $0 \mathrel{\&\&} \ldots$ has the value 0, and
    $1 \| \ldots$ has the value 1

no matter what the value of the second operand (. . .) is, so here the second operand will not be evaluated. This will save computing time in some cases, but there is a more important aspect. Suppose that we use a machine which halts on a division by zero. Then there is no danger that this should happen if we write

if $(n \mathrel{!=} 0 \mathrel{\&\&} q < k/n) \ldots$

or (equivalently!):

if $(!(n == 0 \| q >= k/n)) \ldots$

Division by zero is just an example. There are many other situations where we can benefit from this behaviour of && and || with respect to the second operand, avoiding nested if-constructs that otherwise would have been necessary. The operator ! is a unary operator, like $-$ in $(-b + a)$. We can often avoid this operator if we wish. Should the equivalence of the last two if-constructs not be immediately clear it will be easy to verify that

$!(a < b)$

has the same value (0 or 1) as

$a >= b$

2.5 BITWISE LOGICAL OPERATORS

The following operators for bit manipulation can be applied to operands of types *int, short, long, unsigned, char*:

    &   bitwise AND
    | bitwise OR
    $\wedge$ bitwise EXCLUSIVE OR
    $\ll$ left shift
    $\gg$ right shift
    $\sim$ one's complement

For example, the value of $23 \mathbin{\&} 26$ is 18. To understand this, we have to be familiar with the binary number system, where numbers are written as sequences of bits:

$$
\begin{aligned}
23 &= 0 \ldots 0\ 1\ 0\ 1\ 1\ 1 \\
26 &= 0 \ldots 0\ 1\ 1\ 0\ 1\ 0 \\
\hline
18 &= 0 \ldots 0\ 1\ 0\ 0\ 1\ 0
\end{aligned}
\quad \&
$$

In the result of an & operation, each binary position contains a 1-bit only if both operands also have a 1-bit in that position. Analogously, for each position in the result of an | operation we obtain a 0-bit only if both operands also have a 0-bit in that position.

For positive n, the left shift operation

$$i \ll n$$

yields $i \cdot 2^n$ (provided that the latter value is small enough to fit into a machine word used for integers). Similarly, the right-shift operator $\gg$ can be used for integer division by a power of 2.

The unary operator $\sim$ yields the one's complement of its operand. For each 0-bit in the operand, there is a 1-bit in the result, and for each 1-bit in the operand, the corresponding result bit is 0. For example, if the two's complement notation for negative numbers is used, the value of ~ 1 is -2, since then in binary notation we have

$$
\begin{aligned}
1 &= 0 \ldots 0\ 1 \\
-2 &= 1 \ldots 1\ 0
\end{aligned}
$$

2.6 ASSIGNMENT OPERATORS

In the C language a single equal sign ($=$) is an assignment operator, used in assignment expressions such as

$$x = a + b$$

This expression assigns the sum of a and b to x, but it also has this sum as its value, so the following is a valid expression:

$$y = 3 * (x = 5 + (u = 7)) + 1$$

After the execution of this expression we have $u = 7$, $x = 12$, $y = 37$, and the value of the entire expression is 37. If we place a semicolon (;) at the end of an assignment expression, the result is an assignment statement. Thus,

$t = 5$	is an assignment expression;
$t = 5;$	is an assignment statement

Besides $=$, there are some other assignment operators that are used frequently. Instead of the expressions

$$x = x + a \qquad y = y - b \qquad u = u + 1 \qquad v = v - 1$$

we can write

$$x += a \qquad\qquad y -= b \qquad\qquad ++u \qquad\qquad --v$$

The value of $++u$ is the incremented value of u, so first u is incremented and then its value is used. The opposite order is also possible. If we write

$u++$

the old value of u is used first and u is incremented afterwards. So after the execution of

$u = 5; \quad v = 5; \quad x = ++u; \quad y = v++;$

we have $u = v = x = 6$, and $y = 5$. Note that we can also write the statements (with semicolon!)

$u++;$

and

$++u;$

They both have the effect that u is incremented by 1. Here the values of the expressions $u++$ and $++u$ (written without semicolons!) are not used, so these two statements are equivalent.

2.7 RULES FOR PRECEDENCE AND ASSOCIATIVITY

All operators of the C language are listed below, according to decreasing precedence. Those occurring on one line have the same precedence. Some of these operators are not yet discussed, but for later purposes a complete list is given. Unless indicated otherwise, all operators associate from left to right. What this means will be explained presently.

```
( )   [ ]   →   .
!   ~   ++   --   -   (type)   *   &   sizeof
                          (these are unary operators,
                          associating from right
                          to left)

*   /   %
+   -   (binary)
«   »
<   >   <=   >=
==   !=
&
^
|
&&
||
?:   (this operator associates from right to left)
=   +=   -=   *=   /=   %=   «=   »=   &=   ^=   |=
(assignment operators, associating from right to left)
,
```

Most operators associate from left to right. This means that, for example,

$100 - 20 - 1 + 3$

should be interpreted as

$((100 - 20) - 1) + 3$

If it were computed as

$100 - (20 - (1 + 3))$

(which is not the case!) we would have said that the operators associate from right to left. Though rather artifical,

$-!++u$

is valid and means

$-(!(++u))$

since all unary operators associate from right to left. More realistically, we can write

$x = y = z = 7$

which means

$x = (y = (z = 7))$

Here, too, association is from right to left, as the nested parentheses clearly show.

For those who are familiar with Fortran or Pascal the following comparison of notations for some operators may be helpful:

Fortran	Pascal	C
$=$	$:=$	$=$
$.EQ.$	$=$	$==$
$.NE.$	$<>$	$!=$
$.LT.$	$<$	$<$
$.GT.$	$>$	$>$
$.LE.$	$<=$	$<=$
$.GE.$	$>=$	$>=$
$.AND.$	and	$\&\&$
$.OR.$	or	$\|\|$
$.NOT.$	not	$!$
$/$	$/$ div	$/$

2.8 TYPE-CONVERSION

There are many situations where some type is given in a context where a different type would be more appropriate. Let us, for example, assume that we have declared:

short x_short;
int x_int;
long x_long;

unsigned x_unsigned;
float x_float;
double x_double;
char x_char;

The question now arises whether, for example,

x_int = x_float

is a valid assignment. The answer to this question is in the affirmative, but we should be aware that truncation will take place. It is recommended to replace the last assignment with

x_int = (int) x_float

Here the keyword *int* between parentheses is a so-called *cast*-operator. Such cast-operators enable us to prescribe a conversion to a target data type, independent of the context. So

(int) x_float

is of type int. In an assignment a cast-operator could be omitted without altering the effect, but there are other situations where it must not be omitted. Suppose that we wish to print the value of *x_int* as a float number in eight positions with two decimals. This must not be written as

printf ("%8.2f", x_int)

but

printf ("%8.2f", (float) x_int)

is acceptable. The cast operator *(float)* is also useful if truncation is to be prevented in a division. Suppose that *x_int* is to be divided by another integer, say *y_int,* and the exact quotient is to be assigned to *x_float.*
This must not be written

x_float = x_int / y_int;

since that would imply truncation to an integer quotient which is subsequently converted to type float. (Recall that / always yields an integer result if there are two integer operands.) Here a cast-operator should be used at least once:

x_float = (float) x_int / (float) y_int;   or
x_float = (float) x_int / y_int;   or
x_float = x_int / (float) y_int;

Conversion from float to double, caused by

(double) x_float

works as we expect, and so does conversion from double to float:

(float) x_double

Obviously, it is inevitable that some loss of precision will occur in the latter case.

The types float and double are collectively called *floating* types. Similar rules apply to conversion between the types short, int, long, unsigned, char. These types are closely related to each other and are collectively called *integral* types. In these conversions zero bits are added on the left, or left-hand bits are simply omitted.

Suppose that we have the following internal data formats:

long   32 bits
short   16 bits

Then

$x\_long = 0X12345678;$
$x\_short = (short)\ x\_long;$

will be equivalent to

$x\_long = 0X12345678;$
$x\_short = 0X5678;$

(If in the former statements the cast-operator were omitted, the result would be the same.)

The types int and char are so closely related that in practice we often omit cast-operators for these conversions, writing, for example:

$x\_int = x\_char;$

Probably on all machines the statement

$x\_char = 'A' + 1;$

will have the same effect as:

$x\_char = 'B';$

Type *unsigned* is used if the leftmost bit should be regarded as a value-bit rather than as a sign bit. Unsigned and int objects have the same length. If unsigned is converted to long by

$(long)\ x\_unsigned$

zeros are added on the left.

2.9 CONDITIONAL EXPRESSIONS AND IF-STATEMENTS

The character pair ?: forms a very useful operator. With three given expressions we can build a new expression:

$expression\_1\ ?\ expression\_2 : expression\_3$

An example is

$a < b\ ?\ b - a : a - b$

The value of this conditional expression is

$b - a$ if a is less than b, or
$a - b$ if a is not less than b

In the general form above, either *expression_2* or *expression_3* is evaluated, depending on the truth or falsehood of *expression_1*. (Recall that 0 is the code for false and that any non-zero value means true in a logical context.)

We often require that the execution of some statement should depend on a condition. (Instead of *condition* we shall use the more general term *expression*.) For this purpose we use an if-statement of the form:

> *if (expression) statement_1*

We can also use the following extended form of the if-statement:

> *if (expression) statement_1 else statement_2*

The parentheses that surround the expression are mandatory. Remember that the keyword *then* of some other languages is not used in C! If the value of the expression is non-zero, *statement_1* is executed. In the extended if-statement, *statement_2* is executed if the value of the expression is 0. Here are four examples of if-statements:

```
if (x < 0) x = -x;
if (u < 0)v = -u; else v = u;
if (n == 100) { n = 0; k++; }
if (a >= b)
{ p = 0;
   q = 1;
} else
{ s = 100;
   t = 200;
}
```

Since a semicolon really belongs to an assignment statement, it cannot be omitted before *else* in the second example. Notice that we can replace this second example with one assignment statement containing a conditional expression:

> $v = (u < 0 ? -u : u);$

(Since ?: has higher precedence than =, the parentheses in this expression could be omitted.)

In the third example we have introduced a *compound statement,* which has the form

> { *statement statement . . . statement* }

A compound statement groups together several statements into one. It can then be used in contexts where only one statement is allowed. We write two braces belonging to one another either on the same (horizontal) line or in the same (vertical) column. In the latter case we indent the statements within the braces, as shown in the last if-statement. In this way we keep our programs as readable as possible, even in more complex situations where compound statements are nested, as, for example, in:

```
if (a >= b)
{ x = 0;
   if (a >= b + 1)
   { xx = 0;
      yy = -1;
   } else
   { xx = 100;
      yy = 200;
   }
} else
{ x = 1;
   xx = -100;
   yy = 0;
}
```

If we are very economical with braces (which is unwise) an additional rule will be needed to solve an ambiguity with respect to the keyword *else*. This rule says that if two keywords *if* are candidates to belong to a certain keyword *else,* the nearest is the right one. Thus the nested if-statement

if $(a == b)$ *if* $(c == d)$ $x = 1$; *else* $x = 2$;

is to be read as

if $(a == b)$ { *if* $(c == d)$ $x = 1$; *else* $x = 2$; }

Of course, the braces in the latter line increase readability, so in cases like this we had better use them.

If-statements are examples of statements that contain other statements: in other words, statements may be nested. Because of this, it does not make sense to use the number of statements as a measure of the length of a C program.

If an if-statement ends with a compound statement its last character is a brace. This brace is not followed by a semicolon. Only certain statements, for example assignment statements, end with a semicolon. In C semicolons should not be regarded as statement separators, since they belong to the statements themselves.

2.10 REPETITION STATEMENTS; THE COMMA-OPERATOR

The C language offers the following three special constructions for loops:

(1) The while-statement;
(2) The for-statement;
(3) The do-while-statement.

A *while-statement* has the form:

while (*expression*) *statement*

An example is

$$while \ (b \ != 0) \ \{ \ p = p + a; b = b - 1; \ \}$$

which, incidentally, an experienced C programmer would never write in this form. Instead he will probably use

$$while \ (b) \ \{ \ p += a; b--; \ \}$$

This is executed as follows. First it is tested whether the value of b is non-zero. If so, p is increased by a, and b is decremented by one. Then the value of b is tested again, and so on. If in such a test b turns out to be zero, the execution of the while statement is completed.

To introduce the for-statement we first consider the following while-statement preceded by an assignment statement:

$$i = 1;$$
$$while \ (i <= n) \ \{ \ s += i; i++; \ \}$$

The effect of this program fragment can also be achieved by:

$$for \ (i = 1; i <= n; i++) \ s += i;$$

In more abstract (but not less precise!) terms, we can replace

*expression*_1;
while (*expression*_2) { *statement expression*_3 }

with the *for-statement*

for (*expression*_1; *expression*_2; *expression*_3) *statement*

Check that we obtain our last two concrete program fragments if we choose

*expression*_1:	$i = 1$
*expression*_2:	$i <= n$
*expression*_3:	$i++$
statement:	$s += i;$

The third loop construction is the *do-while-statement*. It has the general form

do statement while (*expression*);

An example is:

$$do \ \{ \ s += i; i++; \ \} \ while \ (i <= n);$$

As the notation suggests, here the test for loop-termination (or rather loop-continuation!) is carried out *after* execution of the inner part of the loop. (Recall that both the while-statement and the for-statement perform this test at the beginning of the loop). In our last example this means that s is updated at least once, even if before execution of this do-while-statement i and n are given the values 1 and 0, respectively.

In the above examples rather complex statements were written on one line. Such compact notations have the advantage that, when working with the computer, a substantial portion of a large program will be visible on the screen, or on a single page. On the other hand, if a compound statement is too large for one line, we had better use indentation in a way similar to that shown for the if-statement. For the three types of repetition statements we shall indent as follows:

while (. . .)
{ . . .
  . . .
}
for (. . . ; . . . ; . . .)
{ . . .
  . . .
  . . .
}
do
{ . . .
  . . .
  . . .
} *while* (. . .);

In a statement of the form

  expression;

we may omit the expression, leaving only the semicolon, as a so-called *null statement*. Using this, we can write a very simple infinite loop as

  while (1) ;

or, almost as simple, as

  do ; *while*(1);

Furthermore, each of the three expressions in

  for (*expression*_1; *expression*_2; *expression*_3)

may be omitted, so another infinite loop is

  for (; ;) ;

We can also omit only one or two of these expressions.

Suppose, for example, that the variable i has been assigned a value previously. If we now wish to update this variable in a complicated way inside the loop, and to continue as long as i is positive, we could write something of the form

  for (; $i > 0$;)
  { . . .
    . . .
    . . .
  }

In many situations, especially in connection with loops, we can benefit from the *comma*-operator. It appears in the form

$$expression\_1, \ expression\_2$$

which is a new expression. Its evaluation simply consists of evaluating *expression*_1 and *expression*_2, in that order. An example is

> *while (ch = getchar( ), ch >='0' && ch <= '9') xxx*

where *xxx* is some statement. (With *getchar( )* we read a character from the keyboard, as will be discussed in Section 2.12.) The same effect can be achieved by

> *while ((ch = getchar( )) >= '0' && ch <= '9') xxx*

or, less briefly, by

```
ch = getchar( );
while (ch >= '0' && ch <= '9') { xxx ch = getchar( ); }
```

Another application of the comma-operator is the following for-loop, where we have two 'controlled variables' *i* and *j*, the former increasing and the latter decreasing:

> *for (i = 0, j = N − 1; i < N; i++, j−−) xxx*

2.11 *BREAK, CONTINUE, SWITCH, GOTO*

The statement

> *break*;

terminates the (innermost) loop that contains this statement. We can use it in each of the three types of repetition statements. It provides another means to place a termination test in the middle of a loop. For example, in

```
while (1)
{ ch = getchar( );
   if (ch == '+') break;
   . . .
}
```

the character read by *getchar( )* is processed only if it is not a plus sign, so the whole construction is equivalent to

> *while (ch = getchar( ), ch != '+') . . .*

or

> *while ((ch = getchar( )) != '+') . . .*

Also, the statement

> *continue*;

can be used in each of the three loop types. It causes a jump to the test for termination. For example,

```
while (i < n)
{ i++; . . .
   if (i * i < s)
   { . . .

     . . .

   }
}
```

can also be written as:

```
while (i < n)
{ i++; . . .
   if (i * i >= s) continue;

   . . .

   . . .

}
```

The *switch-statement* serves to jump to some computed position. Its general form is:

switch (expression) statement

Usually the *statement* at the end of this construction is a compound statement, containing several occurrences of the keyword *case* and, at most, one occurrence of the keyword *default.* The switch-statement then has the form:

```
switch (expression)
{ case constant: statement . . . statement
   case constant: statement . . . statement

   . . .

   default: statement . . . statement
}
```

The expression is evaluated and compared with the constants. These 'constants' may in fact be so-called *constant-expressions,* in which no variables occur. Their values must be distinct and of integral type. If the *expression* has the same value as one of the constants, control is transferred to the first statement after that constant. If not, control is transferred to the first statement after *default,* if there is one. If no case matches and there is no default, no action is performed. The default case may occur anywhere among the other cases, not only at the end, as above.

The following example computes the value of the variable *d.* It is the number of days that there are left in a non-leap year, counted from the beginning of a given month m $(1 \leqslant m \leqslant 12)$:

```
d = 0;
switch (m)
```

```
{ case  1: d += 31;
  case  2: d += 28;
  case  3: d += 31;
  case  4: d += 30;
  case  5: d += 31;
  case  6: d += 30;
  case  7: d += 31;
  case  8: d += 31;
  case  9: d += 30;
  case 10: d += 31;
  case 11: d += 30;
  case 12: d += 31;
}
```

For example, if $m = 1$, d is first increased by 31, then by 28, and so on, until finally we have $d = 365$.

The case-prefix

case constant:

may occur more than once before a sequence of statements. This is used in the following example, which also shows that the statement after *switch*(...) need not be a compound statement:

```
switch (telephone_number)
      case 398474: case 987619: case 730488:
      telephone_number = 844564;
```

This switch-statement has the same effect as the following if-statement.

```
if (telephone_number == 398474 ||
    telephone_number == 987619 ||
    telephone_number == 730488) telephone_number = 844564;
```

It is often necessary to jump out of the switch-statement as soon as the statements of the matching case have been executed. To this end we use the break-statement in the same way as we used it to jump out of a loop. An example is:

```
switch (ch)
{ case 'N': case 'n': printf("New York"); break;
  case 'L': case 'l': printf("London"); break;
  case 'A': case 'a': printf("Amsterdam"); break;
  default: printf("invalid code"); break;
}
```

If *ch* has been given the value '*L*' (or '*l*') the effect of this switch-statement is that

London

will be printed. If the break-statements had been omitted, $ch = 'L'$ would have led to the wrong result

LondonAmsterdaminvalid code

(Only the last *break,* immediately preceding the final brace, can always be omitted without altering the effect of the switch-statement.)

Thus, in general, the break-statement causes termination of the smallest enclosing while, for, do-while, or switch-statement.

According to modern programming standards, using the following statement should be avoided. It is mentioned only for the sake of completeness. We can unconditionally jump to some labelled statement by

> *goto label*;

where *label* is an identifier to label some statement in the same function. For example, instead of

```
while (1)
{ ch = getchar( );
  if (ch >= '+') break;
  . . .
}
xxx
```

we can write

```
again:
    ch = getchar( );
    if (ch >= '+') goto ready;
    . . .
    goto again;
ready:
    xxx
```

Though this might seem reasonable, in large programs goto-statements often lead to programming errors, and when they do not, they usually reduce our ability to understand how those programs work.

2.12 BASIC I/O FACILITIES

Since we wish to write useful programs as soon as possible we can no longer postpone a preliminary discussion of input and output (I/O). At this stage we restrict ourselves to input from the keyboard and output to the screen of our terminal (or computer).

We begin with a single character. This can be read from the keyboard into the char variable *ch* by either

> *ch = getchar( )*

or

> *scanf("%c", &ch)*

(The notation *&ch* of the second argument will be discussed shortly.) Analogously, the value of that variable can be written on our terminal screen by either

> *putchar(ch)*

or

printf ("%c", ch)

(In Chapter 6 we shall see that actually *ch* is often declared as *int* rather than as *char,* when used in connection with *getchar* and *putchar.*)

The four above forms are expressions. Together with an immediately following semicolon they form statements. For example,

ch = getchar( )   is an expression
ch = getchar( );   is a statement

For reasons to be explained later, if we use *getchar* or *putchar,* the following line must be placed at the beginning of our program.

#include ⟨stdio. h⟩

The following program counts how many occurrences of the letter *E* (or *e*) appear in a piece of text read from the keyboard. A plus sign signals the end of the input data. Just to demonstrate the use of *putchar,* the characters *A* to *Z* are then printed. (Instead of 'the characters *A* to *Z*' it seems more natural to speak about 'the upper-case alphabet'. If our computer uses the ASCII character set, this is indeed an equivalent phrase. There are, however, other character sets, for example EBCDIC, where the range *A* to *Z* contains more characters than only the 26 capital letters.)

```
#include ⟨stdio. h⟩
main ( )
{ char ch; int n = 0;
  printf ("Input text (terminated by +): \n");
  while (ch = getchar( ), ch != '+')
     if (ch == 'E' || ch == 'e') n++;
  printf ("\nOutput: \n");
  printf ("The above text contains %d occurrences\
  of E and e. \n", n);
  printf ("Characters A to Z: \n");
  for (ch = 'A'; ch <= 'Z'; ch++) putchar(ch);
  putchar('\n');
}
```

If the letters *A* to *Z* form a consecutive sequence in the character set of the machine, we can execute this program with input and output as shown below:

Input text (terminated by +):
This is some piece of text
to count the letter E (or e).
+
Output:
The above text contains 9 occurrences of E and e.
Characters A to Z:
ABCDEFGHIJKLMNOPQRSTUVWXYZ

As this program shows, we can write a character string on several lines by using a backslash \ at the end of a line. The string is then continued on the next line, as if we had written it on one program line.

Both *scanf* and *printf* are functions with arguments. Their first argument is a format string, which gives information about the external representation of the data to be read or written. In addition to this, a format string for *printf* can also contain characters that are to be written literally. The format string is usually followed by other arguments, which we call *data items*. Thus we have

scanf(format_string, data_item1, data_item2, ...)
printf(format_string, data_item1, data_item2, ...)

The format string must contain a conversion specification for each data item. Each conversion specification begins with a per cent character and ends with a conversion character. The first conversion specification belongs to the first data item, and so on. Here we discuss the conversion characters *d, f* and *c*, occurring in the following example:

int i = 12; float x = 1.23456789; char ch = '?';
printf("%4d%7.4f%c", i, x, ch);

This gives the following output:

^^12^1.2346?

where ^ stands for a space. Format item %4d says that the value of integer *i* is to be printed decimally in four positions. As a result of %7.4f, the (floating-point) value *x* will be printed in seven positions with four (rounded) decimals after the point. We can also use the simpler forms %d and %f instead of %4d and %7.4f. The numbers are then printed in as many digits as are needed, with six decimals after the point for floating-point values. In this case we have to use at least one space between the format items, which will then literally appear in the outputs, to prevent all digits being printed as one long number. If we again denote a space by ^, and use the same values of *i, x, ch*, the statement

printf("%d   %f   %c", i, x, ch);

prints

12^1.234568^?

but

printf("%d%f%c", i, x, ch);

would print

121.234568?

In practice, we often wish to print literal text along with the values of the data items. In particular, a format string often ends with the newline character \n. An example is

printf("i = %d   x = %f   ch = %c\n", i, x, ch);

which, in the above context, produces the output line

$i = 12$ $x = 1.234568$ $ch = ?$

The conversion character f can be used both for float and for double data items because it is a general rule that float arguments are implicitly converted to double before they are passed to functions. So for float x,

printf ("%f", x);

is interpreted as

printf ("%f", (double)x);

In other words, the conversion character f expects a data item of type double, and this is provided for, even if a float data item is given. However, integral types are not automatically converted to double, so %f must not be used for an integral data item, and neither can %d correspond to a floating data item. In our previous examples, %c takes care that *ch* is printed as a single character. If we had written %d instead of %c, the internal integer value of the character would have been printed.

With *scanf* things are somewhat different, which should not surprise us, since input is essentially different from output. With *printf* the data items could be any arithmetic expressions, but *scanf* has to know the locations where it is to store the values of the data that are read, so clearly an expression like

$i * (j + k)$

cannot be used as argument. The positions of those locations in memory are called *addresses*. It is the addresses of the variables that have to be passed as arguments. In C this is very clearly reflected in the notation by using the unary operator &, which can be read as *the address of*. An example is:

int i; float x; double xx; char ch;
scanf ("%d %f %lf %c", &i, &x, &xx, &ch);

Instead of *address of* we often say *pointer to*, so &i is an expression whose value is a pointer to i. Its type is said to be *pointer-to-int*. In our discussion of *printf* we noted that float arguments of functions are automatically converted to type double. However, a similar conversion does not take place with the corresponding pointer types, so pointer-to-float is not implicitly converted to pointer-to-double. The types of &x and &xx are therefore essentially different, which is to be reflected in the corresponding conversion specifications. This is why we have to write %lf for a corresponding pointer-to-double data item, as the example shows. Remember that for double precision *xx* we write

printf ("%f", xx)   but
scanf ("%lf", &xx)

In the format string of *scanf* blank spaces between format specifications are ignored. Other characters require the same characters to appear in the input, so

scanf ("Q%d", &n)

expects the letter Q to appear before the value for n. In Section 4.4 we shall see that any value returned by a function may be either used or ignored, whichever we like. An example of this is *scanf*. If it is certain that a number can be read we can ignore the returned value, which, incidentally, is equal to the number of items that have been read. However, we can also use the returned value to test whether the read attempt has been successful. For example, if a single character and two numbers are to be read there are three data items, so the following construction makes sense:

> *if (scanf("%c %d %f", &ch, &n, &x) < 3) { ... /* error */ }*

Another useful application of the value returned by *scanf* is to signal the logical end of a sequence of numbers which, one at a time, are read in a loop. We can simply place a special character such as # after the last number, causing *scanf* to fail when attempting to read a number. For example, the sum of the numbers in the following input line:

> 10 20 30 #

can be computed as follows:

> *sum = 0.0;*
> *while (scanf("%f", &x)) sum += x;*

Here the fourth call of *scanf* will result in the function value 0, which, as we know, is interpreted as *false*.

When reading input data we sometimes feel the need to find out what the next character will be. We can then read this character and subsequently place it back into the input stream. For the keyboard, we place the value of character variable *ch* back as follows:

> *ungetc(ch, stdin);*

A subsequent call of *getchar* will then yield the same character. The identifier *stdin* denotes a so-called *file pointer*, which we shall discuss in Section 6.2. Example 1 in the next section shows how we can use *ungetc*.

2.13 EXAMPLES

Example 1

Compute the sum of an unknown number of integers read from the keyboard. The last integer is immediately followed by the character #. Any negative numbers should also be read properly if its minus sign immediately follows the preceding number. Here is a solution:

```
/* SUM: This program computes the sum of a sequence of
          integers.                                          */
#include <stdio. h>
main ( )
```

```
{ int i, s = 0;
  char ch;
  printf("Enter a sequence of integers,\n");
  printf("(The last integer must immediately\n");
  printf("be followed by the character #): \n");
  while (ch = getchar( ), ch != '#')
  { ungetc(ch, stdin);
    scanf("%d", &i); s += i;
  }
  printf("\nThe sum is %d\n", s);
}
```

The program can be used as follows:

Enter a sequence of integers.
(The last integer must immediately
be followed by the character #):
50 20–3
10 100#

The sum is 177

Although numbers are usually separated by blanks, we have omitted a blank between the numbers 20 and −3. After the number 20 has been read, the next character must be read to determine whether or not it is the endcode #. As this turns out not to be the case, the minus sign is put back into the input stream by means of *ungetc(ch, stdin)*, so that −3 will be the next number that is read.

Example 2

Write a program similar to our first program *NVALUE* in the introduction, but now, instead of 5, we use M in

$$1 + \frac{1}{2} + \frac{1}{3} + \ldots + \frac{1}{n} \geqslant M$$

where M is variable. The program is to read the maximum value M_{max} and M will successively have the values $1, 2, \ldots, M_{max}$. Again we want the smallest n that satisfies each inequality. (Readers familiar with classical mathematics will perhaps know that for large M the following value n' is a good approximation of n:

$$n' = e^{M - C}$$

where

$$C = 0.57721566490\ldots = \text{Euler's constant}$$

We will not use this knowledge in our program.)

For each next value of M we shall use what we have computed before, since it would be a waste of computing time if we started with $1 + 1/2 + \ldots$ for each new sum. Here is the program:

```
/* NVALUES: Compute the smallest n satisfying
                  1 + 1/2 + . . . + 1/n >= M,
                  for M = 1, 2, . . . , Mmax         */
main( )
{ int n = 0, M, Mmax; double s = 0.0;
  printf("Largest value of M?");
  scanf("%d", &Mmax);
  printf(" M      n\n");
  for (M = 1; M <= Mmax; M++)
  { while (s < M) s += 1.0 / ++n;
    printf("%2d %9d\n", M, n);
  }
}
```

Notice the concisely written while-statement. In most other languages a probably less efficient notation, equivalent to

$$while\ (s < M)\ \{\ n = n + 1;\ s = s + 1.0/n;\ \}$$

would be required.

If program NVALUES is executed with 10 as the maximum value for M, the output will be as shown below.

```
Largest value of M? 10
M        n
1        1
2        4
3        11
4        31
5        83
6        227
7        616
8        1674
9        4550
10       12367
```

Example 3

Write a program which reads a sequence of real numbers and determines their average and their smallest and largest values. The character # after the last number signals the end of the sequence. For example, the sequence

8 20 7 5 #

should lead to the following output:

```
Average:      10.000000
Minimum:       5.000000
Maximum:      20.000000
```

Here is the program:

```
/* STATISTICS: This program computes the average and the minimum and
     maximum value of a sequence of non-negative real numbers.   */
main( )
{ float x, sum = 0.0, min, max; int n = 0;
  printf ("Enter a number sequence, followed by #: \n");
  while (scanf ("%f", &x))
  { sum +=x; n++;
    if (n == 1) min = max = x; else
    if (x < min) min = x; else
    if (x > max) max = x;
  }
  if (n == 0) printf ("Empty sequence\n"); else
  printf ("Average: %16.6f\nMinimum: %16.6f\nMaximum: %16.6f\n",
        sum/n,              min,                 max);
}
```

Note the nested if-statement in the middle of this program. Each statement in

if (expression) statement else statement

can again be an if-statement. In program *STATISTICS* this principle is applied twice. The numbers read by *scanf* can be typed in free format. Between each two numbers, a space, a newline character, a tab or several of these characters can occur.

Example 4

We want a program which reads a piece of text from the keyboard. The program has to count the number of input lines and to determine the length of the longest of these lines. Each line consists of a number of readable ASCII characters, followed by a newline character, which must not be included when counting characters. A dollar sign ($) at the very beginning of a line signals the end of the input. (The count of input lines should not include this final line.)

SOLUTION

```
/* LINECOUNT: This program counts the number of lines read from the
     keyboard. It also determines the length of the longest of those lines.   */
#include ⟨stdio. h⟩
main( )
{ char ch; int n = 0, len, maxlen = 0;
  printf ("Give lines of text. A line beginning with $\n");
  printf ("signals the end of the input. \n\n");
  while (ch = getchar( ), ch != '$')
  { len = 0; n++;
    while (ch != '\n') { len++; ch = getchar( ); }
    if (len > maxlen) maxlen = len;
  }
```

printf (*"\nNumber of input lines:* %3*d\n", n*);
if (*n* > 0)
    printf (*"Maximum line length:*   %3*d\n", maxlen*);
}

The last if-statement takes care that no line length is printed if the number of lines is zero. Here is a demonstration of this program:

Give lines of text. A line beginning with $
signals the end of the input.

This is some piece of
text closed by $ at the
beginning of
a line.
$

Number of input lines: 4
Maximum line length: 23

Example 5

Write a program which reads one line. At most, four decimal digits on this line are to be assembled to an integer number. As soon as four digits have been read, the remaining characters can be ignored. Thus for the line

*ABCD*3.4   *EF* 5 *GH*6932*I*

the required number is 3456. If the line contains no digits at all, the resulting number should be zero. Here is the program:

```
/* COMPOSE: A line is read from the keyboard, and the first four digits are
                    assembled to one integer.   */
#include ⟨stdio. h⟩
main( )
{ int num = 0, n = 0, digit; char ch;
   printf ("Give a line of text: \n\n");
   while (ch = getchar( ), ch != '\n')
   { if (ch >= '0' && ch <= '9')
      { n++; digit = ch − '0'; num = 10 * num + digit;
        if (n == 4) break;
      }
   }
   printf ("\nThe first four digits form the number: %d\n", num);
}
```

Example 6

Write a program which reads two non-negative integer numbers *a* and *b* and a positive number *n*. The last *n* digits of *a* + *b* are to be printed with a space between each two adjacent digits. Leading zeros need not be suppressed, so exactly *n* digits will be printed. For example, if a, b, n have the values 27, 6989, 3, respectively, we have $a + b = 7016$, and the output will be

    0 1 6

We shall assume that no integer overflow will occur when $a + b$ is computed, or when 10 is raised to the power n.

SOLUTION

```
/* DECOMPOSE: The last n digits of a + b are printed digit by digit. The
                 integers a, b and n are given.   */
#include ⟨stdio. h⟩
main( )
{ int a, b, n, s, tenpower, num, i, digit;
  printf ("Give a, b and n:"); scanf ("%d %d %d", &a, &b, &n);
  s = a + b; tenpower = 1;
  for (i = 0; i < n; i++) tenpower *= 10;
  num = s % tenpower;
  for (i = 0; i < n; i++)
  { tenpower /= 10; digit = num / tenpower; num %= tenpower;
    putchar('0' + digit); putchar(i < n − 1 ? ' ' : '\n');
  }
}
```

2.14 EXERCISES

2.1 The following program contains four statements which either lead to error messages or print unpredictable values. Remove them and predict the output of the revised program. Run the program on a computer to verify your predictions. Be careful.

```
main( )
{ int i = 2;
  printf ("%d\n", 8 * i / 3);
  printf ("%d\n", 8.0 * i);
  printf ("%f\n", 8 * i);
  printf ("%f\n", 8 * i / 3);
  printf ("%d\n", 8 * i % 3);
  printf ("%f\n", 8.0 * i % 3);
  printf ("%d\n", i > 4 ? 10 : 15);
  printf ("%d\n", i = 4 ? 10 : 15);
}
```

2.2 Write a program which reads the number n, followed by a sequence of n integers. Check whether this sequence contains at least two different integers, and if so, determine the second least integer of the sequence.

2.3 As Exercise 1.2, but now the very first number n is not given. Instead, the character # follows the last number.

2.4 Write a program which reads a sequence of characters. To signal the end, the plus sign is used. Count how many of these characters are decimal digits. At the same time, compute the sum of these digits.

2.5 Write a program which reads lines of text. A question mark (?) at the beginning of a line signals the end. Count how many lines have a period (.) as their last character.

2.6 Write a program which reads words of letters $(A, \ldots, Z, a, \ldots, z)$, separated by blanks, newlines and punctuation characters (. , ? ;). An empty line is the end of the input. Count how many words are read.

2.7 Write a program to print a 'checker-board' which has $2n^2$ black fields, each consisting of $k \times k$ asterisks. The numbers n and k have to be read. For example, if $n = 2$ and $k = 3$, the output is as follows:

CHAPTER 3

Arrays and pointers

3.1 ARRAYS

The array declaration

> *int a*[1000];

reserves memory for 1000 integer variables, which are written as

> *a*[0], *a*[1], . . . , *a*[999].

We have access to these variables in any order we like, and we can use them in the same way as simple integer variables. For example, we can write

> *a*[831] = 2; *a*[15] = 3; *printf*("%d", *a*[831] * *a*[15] + 1);

which will print 7. Instead of constants as 831, any integer expression can be used as a subscript. For example, the for-statement

> *for* (*i* = 200; *i* <= 215; *i* + =5) *a*[*i*] = 10 * *i*;

has the same effect on array *a* as

> *a*[200] = 2000; *a*[205] = 2050; *a*[210] = 2100; *a*[215] = 2150;

In the array declaration the number of elements (here, 1000) has to be specified as a constant. However, this constant need not necessarily be written as a sequence of digits. It is generally considered good programming practice to use *named constants* for this purpose. In the C language named constants are defined by a *#define* preprocessor control line. For example, we can write

> *#define LEN* 1000
> . . .
> *int a*[*LEN*];
> . . .
> *for* (*i* = 0; *i* < *LEN*; *i* + +) *a*[*i*] = 1;

In this example the #define-line has the effect that *LEN* can be used as another notation for 1000. However, *LEN* cannot be used as a variable. Should we write

> *LEN* = 2 * *LEN* + 1;

then this is interpreted as

> 1000 = 2 * 1000 + 1;

which is nonsense. Generally speaking, named constants make a program easier to read and to modify. We shall return to #define-lines in Section 4.8.

Remember, an array subscript in C always counts from zero, so the highest subscript value is one less than the number of elements. Thus in our example

$a[LEN-1]$

is the last element of array a.

Besides int, array elements can have other types, as the following example shows:

```
#define CH_LEN 80
#define FL_LEN 100
. . .
char str[CH_LEN], line[CH_LEN];
float x[FL_LEN];
. . .
x[0] = 3.141592; line[CH_LEN − 1] = '+';
```

3.2 POINTERS

For each variable there is a piece of memory where the variable is stored. Such a memory-location has a number, called its address. For example, as a result of

$int\ i=10,\ j=20,\ k=30;$

the situation in memory might be as follows:

Variable	Address	Value
i	1001	10
j	1002	20
k	1003	30

In the C language not only the value but also the address of a variable is available to the programmer. The notation for the address of i is $\&i$. So in the above example the expressions $\&i$, $\&j$, $\&k$ would have the values 1001, 1002, 1003, respectively. The character $\&$ is a unary operator, and $\&i$ is an expression whose value is said to point to i. For the inverse operation we have the unary operator $*$, to be read as 'the object pointed to by'. For example, $*(\&i)$ is equivalent to i, since it is the object pointed to by $\&i$. Though not very practical, we can write

$*\&i = 10;$

instead of

$i = 10;$

(Note that $*\&i$ means $*(\&i)$, because unary operators associate from right to left.)

In the above example,

i	has type int,
$\&i$	has type pointer-to-int,
$*\&i$	has type int.

The expression $\&i$ is not a variable, so we cannot assign a value to it. However, we can declare a variable of the same type as $\&i$ in the following way:

> *int* $*p$;

This is very reasonable, since it says $*p$ has type int, so p has type pointer-to-int. Extending our previous example, we can now write

> $p = \&i$;

which assigns the address of i to p, so in memory the situation may now be as follows:

Variable	Address	Value
i	1001	10
j	1002	20
k	1003	30
p	1004	1001

If the statement

> $*p = 40$;

is now executed, the object pointed to by p is given the value 40, so in our example the contents of address 1001 is replaced with 40, as if we had written

> $i = 40$;

This example shows that an object in memory can be denoted in various ways. The left-hand side of an assignment can be any expression that denotes an object in memory. Such an expression is called an *lvalue*, where l stands for *left*. Of course, 40 and $-i$ are expressions that are not lvalues since they cannot be used as left-hand sides of assignments. Valid lvalues are, for example:

> i
> $*p$
> $* \&i$

Any expression beginning with $*$ is an lvalue, but any expression that begins with $\&$ is not.

3.3 EQUIVALENCE OF ARRAYS AND POINTERS

After the declaration

> *int* $a[1000]$;

the name a denotes a pointer to array element $a[0]$. Thus instead of

> $\&a[0]$

we can simply write

> a

(Note that in the notation $\&a[0]$ the brackets [ ] have higher precedence than $\&$; see Section 2.7.)

More interestingly, we can add an integer to a pointer. By definition $a + i$ is the address of array element $a[i]$. Thus

$$a + i \qquad \text{is equivalent to} \qquad \&a[i]$$
$$*(a + i) \qquad \text{is equivalent to} \qquad a[i]$$

If we declare

$$int \; a[1000], \; *b;$$

all four notations

$$a[i] \qquad a + i \qquad b[i] \qquad b + i$$

are, in principle, correct. Of course, there are differences between a and b. First, b is an lvalue, and a is not, so an assignment of the form

$$a = \ldots$$

is impossible. Second, immediately after this declaration, a points to $a[0]$, but b is undefined. After the valid assignment

$$b = a,$$

however, b also points to array element $a[0]$, which can now also be written as $b[0]$. Moreover, for any positive integer i less than 1000, $b[i]$ means the same as $a[i]$.

It will not immediately be clear that we can benefit from the equivalence of arrays and pointers. In Section 5.3 we shall see that this equivalence enables us to use what we might call *flexible arrays*. At the moment we shall content ourselves with a consequence of this equivalence which is less spectacular but yet of great practical value.

Let us assume that four arrays of characters have been declared, say, by

$$char \; s[80], \; t[80], \; u[80], \; v[80];$$

We now wish to assign a string to array s. This cannot be accomplished by an assignment statement of the form

$$s = \ldots ;$$

since s is not an lvalue. Instead we use the standard function *strcpy* for string copying, as, for example, in

$$strcpy \; (s, \; \textit{"An Advanced Programming Language"});$$

This statement has the same effect as the following sequence of 33 assignment statements:

$$s[0] = 'A';$$
$$s[1] = 'n';$$
$$\ldots$$
$$s[30] = 'g';$$
$$s[31] = 'e';$$
$$s[32] = '\backslash 0';$$

The null character '\0' is always placed at the end of a character string. Standard functions such as *strcpy* use it to detect the logical end of the character sequence. The given string constant is internally coded in the same way as the array *s*. A string constant and an array of characters such as *s* are identical in many respects, including the null character at the logical end. As a result of its declaration the physical length of array *s* is 80. Only the first 33 characters have been used in this example. Since an array of characters has the same type as a string constant it can also be used as the second argument of *strcpy,* as, for example, in:

   strcpy(*t*, *s*);

As a result, the arrays *t* and *s* have identical contents from their beginnings up to the null character. On the basis of all this it seems that the arguments of *strcpy* must be arrays. However, the array names *s*, *t*, *u* are in fact pointers, or, in other words, they denote addresses, and so do string constants. Therefore the arguments of *strcpy* are pointers to characters. Since we can add an integer to a pointer, we can also write

   strcpy(*u*, *s* + 12);

Here *s* + 12 is a pointer to *s*[12], so the copying process starts at this point, and we obtain the same result as if we had written

   strcpy(*u*, *"Programming Language"*);

Pointer arithmetic can also occur in the first argument of *strcpy*. For example, execution of

   strcpy(*v*, *u*); *strcpy*(*v* + 12, *"in C"*);

will now have the same effect as

   strcpy(*v*, *"Programming in C"*);

In Section 4.9 we shall discuss *strcpy* in connection with some related functions. It was introduced here merely to show that the equivalence of arrays and pointers has pleasing consequences.

   Since a string such as *"Programming in C"* is a pointer to the first element of an array of characters we can write

   char * *title*;
   . . .
   title = *"Programming in C"*;

This does not involve character copying! It is merely an assignation of a pointer to a pointer variable.

   Since we can add an integer to a pointer, and since a string is a pointer, we can write such constructions as

   * (*"ABCDEFG"* + 2)

or, equivalently,

   "ABCDEFG"[2],

both having the value *'C'*.

For the sake of completeness we still have to pay attention to the possibility of subtracting something (an integer or a pointer value) from a pointer. After the declarations

$$double\ a[1000],\ *p,\ *q;$$
$$int\ i;$$

the statements

$$p = a + 999;\ q = p - 300;\ i = p - q;$$

are valid. As their result, p and q point to $a[999]$ and $a[699]$, respectively, and i has the value 300. Note that two pointer values can be subtracted, not added.

3.4 MULTI-DIMENSIONAL ARRAYS

In Section 3.3 we used the declaration

$$char\ s[80],\ t[80],\ u[80],\ v[80];$$

The memory reserved by this declaration can be regarded as four lines (or rows), each consisting of 80 positions (or columns). If instead of naming the rows s, t, u, v, we wish to number them 0, 1, 2, 3, we can declare

$$char\ table[4][80];$$

For i ranging from 0 to 3 and j from 0 to 79 the character in row i and column j is denoted by

$$table[i][j]$$

The relationship between, for example, *table* [0] and *table* [0][j] is the same as that between s and $s[j]$. Thus if we use only one subscript we have an array of 80 characters, or, equivalently, a pointer to the first of those 80 characters. Thus

$table[i]$	is equivalent to	$\&table[i][0]$
$*table[i]$	is equivalent to	$table[i][0]$
$*(table[i] + j)$	is equivalent to	$table[i][j]$

and so on.

 If we are already familiar with another language and we start programming in C we should be aware that in C the notations

$$table[i, j] \quad and \quad table[i][j]$$

are not equivalent. If we use the former notation instead of the latter the compiler may not give an error message, since it considers

$$i, j$$

as a valid expression, where the comma operator connects the operands i and j. Thus $table[i, j]$ is regarded as a clumsy notation for $table[j]$, which is a valid pointer-valued expression. So remember, in C each subscript has a bracket pair of its own, and

$$table[i][j]$$

is the correct spelling for the element in row *i* and column *j*. (With fewer brackets the same array element can be written

$$*(table[i]+j), \quad \text{or}$$
$$*(*(table+i)+j)$$

but these expressions are certainly not simpler than the normal array notation.)

Though rarely used, arrays with three of more dimensions are also possible. For example, a collection of five tables, each of the same dimensions and type as before, can be declared and used as follows:

> char *table_list*[5][4][80];
>
> . . . .
>
> . . . *table_list*[h][i][j] . . .

3.5 ARRAYS OF POINTERS

Array elements can be pointers themselves. Suppose that a long one-dimensional array *str* of characters is used to store names. We can then use another array *start*, whose elements are pointers to the first positions of each name. Here is an example:

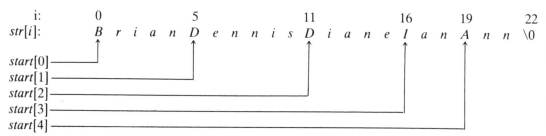

In the following program we actually have this situation.

```
#include ⟨stdio.h⟩
main ( )
{ char str[200], *start[40], *p;
  int j = 0;
  strcpy (str, "BrianDennisDianeIanAnn");
  start[0] = str;
  start[1] = str + 5;
  start[2] = str + 11;
  start[3] = str + 16;
  start[4] = str + 19;
  /* Each name will now be printed on a new line: */
  for (p = str; *p; p++)
  { if (p == start[j]) {putchar('\n'); j++;  }
    putchar(*p);
  }
  putcher ('\n');
}
```

There are some new notations in this program. The declaration

char . . . , ∗start[40], . . .

expresses that ∗*start[j]* will have type char (where *j* is non-negative and less than 40). Since brackets have higher precedence than the unary operator ∗, this means that ∗(*start[j]*) has type char, and that *start[j]* consequently has type pointer-to-char. Thus *start* is indeed an array whose elements are pointers to characters. Since the array name *str* and expressions such as *str* + 5 also denote pointers to characters, the assignment statements

start[0] = str;
start[1] = str + 5;

make sense. In the for-statement the initial value of *p* is *str,* so ∗p is *str[0].* So long as ∗*p* is not the null character, the inner part of the loop is executed. If *p* points to the same position as *start[j]*, we are at the beginning of a new name, so a newline character is inserted before the character ∗*p* is printed. The pointer is incremented by *p*++ and the test on the value ∗*p* is carried out again, and so on. Since '\0' has the value 0, which in a logical context means *false,* the loop terminates as soon as the null character at the end of the list of names is reached. The program produces the following output:

Brian
Dennis
Diane
Ian
Ann

3.6 READING AND WRITING STRINGS

There are several methods to read a string (not surrounded by double quotes) from the keyboard. The most primitive way is to read the characters of the string one by one, using, for example,

ch = getchar( );

or

scanf("%c", &ch)

in a loop. If we wish to read a entire line we can use the function *gets,* to be dealt with in Section 6.6. There is a third method of reading a string, which we shall discuss here. This uses the well-known function *scanf* with a new conversion specification, namely %*s.* When read in this way a string is defined as a sequence of normal characters, surrounded by sequences of white-space characters, the latter term being used for the space, the newline character and the tab character. If *str* is an array of characters we can write

scanf("%s", str)

which causes a skip over any initial white-space characters; then all subsequent input characters are read into array *str* until a white-space character is encountered, which signals the end of the string. Instead of that white-space character, a null character is placed at the end. (The white-space character is the next input character.) Note that it would be a mistake to write &str as the second argument of *scanf*, because *str* is an array, or, in other words, a pointer.

Between % and *s* we may specify the maximum number of characters to be read. For example, if we write

> *scanf("%4s", str)*

and type

> *ABCDEF*

on the keyboard, then the four characters *ABCD* plus a terminating null character are placed into array *str*, and *E* is the next character to be read. If instead we type

> *AB*

(followed by a white-space character) only the characters *A*, *B* and a null character are placed into *str*, so in this case the maximum field width has no effect.

We can also use the conversion character *s* to write a string with *printf*. For example, if we write

> *printf("%s", str)*

the characters in *str* that precede the terminating null character are printed.

Between % and *s* we can insert a minimum field width, which says how many positions are at least to be used. If the string is longer than this field width, the entire string is printed (unless a 'precision' is specified, as will be discussed in Section 6.2). If it is shorter, it is padded on the left with spaces. For strings, padding on the right is usually required, which we can achieve by making the field width negative, writing, for example,

> *printf("%-20s", str)*

3.7 EXAMPLES

Example 1

Write a program which reads ten (real) numbers and computes their average. Then a table consisting of two columns has to be printed. The first column must contains the given numbers. In the second column the values must appear that are formed by subtracting the computed average from the number in the first column.

SOLUTION

> /* *DEVIATIONS*: *This program reads ten numbers, and*
> *computes their deviations from their*
> *average.*   */
>
> #define N 10
> main ( )

```
{ float a[N], s = 0.0, average;
  int i;
  printf("Give %d numbers: \n", N);
  for (i = 0; i < N; i++)
  { scanf("%f", a + i); s + = a[i];
  }
  printf("\nAverage = %9.5f\n\n", average = s/N);
  printf("%15s %19s\n", "a[i]", "a[i] – average");
  for (i = 0; i < N; i++)
  printf("%16.4f %16.5f\n", a[i], a[i] – average);
}
```

The output (and input) of the program can be as shown below:

Give 10 *numbers*:
10 20 30 40 50 60 70 80 90 100

Average = 55.00000

a[i]	a[i] – average
10.0000	−45.00000
20.0000	−35.00000
30.0000	−25.00000
40.0000	−15.00000
50.0000	−5.00000
60.0000	5.00000
70.0000	15.00000
80.0000	25.00000
90.0000	35.00000
100.0000	45.00000

Example 2

Write a program which reads text from the keyboard, and counts how often each of the decimal digits $0, 1, \ldots, 9$ occur in the text. To signal the end, the character # will be used.

SOLUTION

```
/* FREQUENCY: This program determines the frequency of the
               digits 0, 1, ... , 9 in a piece of text.              */
#include ⟨stdio. h⟩
main ( )
{ int count[10], i; char ch;
    for (i = 0; i < 10; i++) count[i] = 0;
    printf("Enter text, ending with #:\n");
    while (ch = getchar( ), ch != '#')
        if (ch > ='0' && ch < ='9') count[ch – '0']++;
    printf("\nDigit     Frequency:\n");
    for (i = 0; i < 10; i++)
        printf(" %d %10d\n", i, count[i]);
}
```

Here is an example of how this program is used:

Enter text, ending with #:
My bank account number is 1144288, and my
telephone number is 61830.
#

Digit	Frequency
0	1
1	3
2	1
3	1
4	2
5	0
6	1
7	0
8	3
9	0

Example 3

Write a program which reads a sequence of 20 integers. Determine whether the last number in the sequence occurred earlier. If so, print *Seen before,* otherwise print *New.* The given numbers are integers. Except for the declaration of an array, use pointer notation throughout the program.

SOLUTION

```
/* SEARCH_1:
    A sequence of 20 numbers is read. The last number is
    searched for in the preceding 19 numbers.            */
main ( )
{ int a[20], *p, last;
  printf("Give 20 integers: \n");
   for (p = a; p < a + 20; p++) scanf("%d", p);
   last = *(a + 19);
   for (p = a; *p != last; p++);
            /* Inner part of loop is empty! */
   printf(p == a + 19 ? "New\n" : "Seen before\n");
}
```

This program is best explained by showing an equivalent version with array notation instead of pointers.

```
/* SEARCH_2:
    A sequence of 20 numbers is read. The last number is
    searched for in the preceding 19 numbers.            */
main ( )
```

```
{ int a[20], i, last;
  printf("Give 20 integers: \n");
  for (i = 0; i < 20; i++) scanf("%d", &a[i]);
  last = a[19];
  for (i = 0; a[i] != last; i++);
          /* Inner part of loop is empty! */
  printf(i == 19 ? "New\n" : "Seen before\n");
}
```

Example 4

Write a program which reads a sequence of, at most, 1000 distinct integers in ascending order. The last integer of the sequence is followed by the character #. Then another integer x is read. Use the efficient method known as *binary search* to look for this last number x in the given sequence. In each step the length of the sequence we are searching is shortened by a factor 2, since, depending on the result of a comparison, either the first or the second half of the sequence dealt with is the new sequence in which, subsequently, we search for x. Counting from 1, print the position where x is found, or the message *Not found* if x does not occur in the sequence. Here is the program:

```
/* BINSEARCH: Binary Search in an array.   */
#define N 1000

main ( )
{ int left, right, middle, n, a[N], x;
  printf("Enter at most %d integers, in ascending order,\
  followed by # :\n", N);
  for (n = 0; n < N && scanf("%d", &x) > 0; n++) a[n] = x;
  /* Now a[0], a[1], . . . , a[n − 1] have been read */
  printf("Enter a number to be looked for in the array: ");
  scanf("%d", &x);
  /* Now follows the binary search:   */
  left = 0; right = n − 1;
  do
  { middle = (left + right)/2;
    if (x <= a[middle]) right = middle − 1;
    if (x >= a[middle]) left = middle + 1;
  } while (left <= right);
  if (x == a[middle]) printf("Found in position %d\n",
  middle + 1); /* Internally we count from 0, hence + 1   */
  else printf("Not found\n");
}
```

3.8 EXERCISES

3.1 Write a program which reads a sequence of, at most, 100 (distinct) integers, each immediately followed by a letter. The character # signals the end of the sequence. Then another integer is read, and on the basis of the given sequence it is to be determined if there is a letter that is associated with that integer. For example, the input data

123*B*   492*M*   7621*C*   4*V*   7*B*   #
492

leads to the output line

Associated with 492 is the letter M

whereas the replacement of the last 492 with 493 would give

No letter is associated with 493.

3.2   Write a program which reads a sequence of ten integers, and then, for each of them, counts how many smaller elements follow. For example, the input sequence

8   10   18   7   5   10   13   8   9   20

will give the following result:

8	2
10	4
18	6
7	1
5	0
10	2
13	2
8	0
9	0
20	0

3.3   Two monotonic non-decreasing sequences of integers are to be read. (A sequence is said to be monotonic non-decreasing if no element of the sequence is followed by a smaller element.) The last number of each sequence is followed by the character #. The two sequences are to be merged into one monotonic non-decreasing sequence. For example, with input

8   15   15   30   100   200   #
1   1   40   50   60   #

the output is

1   1   8   15   15   30   40   50   60   100   200

3.4   Write a program which reads an integer n (not greater than 20) followed by a (square) matrix consisting of n rows and n columns. Determine the smallest matrix element and subtract this number from all matrix elements. The matrix thus obtained is to be printed.

3.5   A given sequence of ten real numbers is to be sorted in increasing order. Use the method known as *straight selection,* which works as follows. First, the smallest element of the sequence is selected and interchanged with the first element. Then only the subsequence starting with the second element still has to be sorted. The smallest element of this subsequence is now selected and interchanged with the second element, and so on. In Sections 4.11 and 6.8 we shall discuss sorting algorithms which are much faster for large sequences.

3.6 Write a program which reads a line consisting of words separated by blanks. The words are to be printed in the same order as they are read, but the letters of each word are to be reversed. For example, the input line

   This is an input line

is to be transformed into

   sihT si na tupni enil

3.7 Write a program which reads a line consisting of words separated by blanks. The words are to be printed in the opposite order, so

   This is an input line

is to be transformed into

   line input an is This

3.8 Write a program to subtract two given calender dates. Each date is given as a number of four digits, for example 0401 for the first of April. Print the number that indicates how many days the latter date falls after the former in a non-leap year. For example,

0101	0102	gives	1
0101	1231	gives	364
1231	0101	gives	−364

3.9 Write a program to count the number of distinct integers that are read. The last number of the sequence is followed by the character #. You may assume that not more than 100 distinct integers will be read, but each integer may occur quite often, so the length of the input sequence is not limited.

3.10 The following contains one incorrect statement. Remove it. What is the output of the thus-corrected program?

```
main ( )
{ char str[10];
  strcpy(str, "ABC");
  printf("%c\n", str[2]);
  printf("%d\n", str[3]);
  printf("%c\n", str);
  printf("%s\n", str);
  printf("%c\n", *(str + 1));
  printf("%s\n", str + 1);
  printf("%c\n", (str + 1)[1]);
}
```

CHAPTER 4

Functions and the program structure

4.1 FUNCTIONS AND CALL-BY-VALUE PARAMETERS

Any C program contains a function whose name is *main,* and program-execution starts at the beginning of this function. In a function another function can be used, and so on. In some languages one distinguishes between procedures and functions, and one has to choose among several types of parameter-passing mechanisms. In the C language we have no such distinctions. There are only functions, and there is only one method of passing arguments, technically referred to as call by value. Curiously enough, this simplicity does not restrict us in achieving all we wish.

For the sake of simplicity we begin with functions that have no parameters at all. Here is a program which uses the function *read_int_number.* This function is used to compute the sum of some integer numbers that are read. We shall assume that the number 0 signals the end of the number sequence:

```
main ( )
{ int i, s = 0;
  printf("Give some integers, followed by the integer 0\n");
  while (i = read_int_number ( )) s += i;
  printf("\nThe sum is %d\n", s);
}

int read_int_number ( )
{ int x;
  scanf("%d", &x);
  return x;
}
```

This program consists of the two functions *main* and *read_int_number.* The latter function returns an int value, which is indicated by writing the keyword int before the function name in the first line of the function. The statement

```
return x;
```

causes the value of *x* to be returned as a function value. It also causes immediate return to the place where the function was used. At the end of a function such a return takes place anyhow, so the above example is not a clear illustration of the latter aspect. In the following situation, however, execution of the return-statement implies that *xxx* is not executed:

```
if ( ... ) return ... ;
xxx
```

Instead of the variable x in the above example any expression (of the same type) can be used. Some people seem to prefer parenthesized expressions here, which is a matter of taste. For example, we may write

> return $a * x + b$;

or

> return $(a * x + b)$;

with the same meaning.

We now return to our sample program. In the assignment

> $i = read\_int\_number$ ( )

the right-hand side is said to be a function *call*. We usually say a function is *called*, rather than *used*. The whole expression is really an assignment, not to be mistaken for a comparison, which would have required a double equal sign $==$. The value of this assignment is the value assigned to i. So long as this value is non-zero it is interpreted as *true*, and s is updated by the statement

> $s += i$;

In our next program we have a function with two parameters. This function, too, has to read an integer value, but here the value of $ax + b$ has to be delivered as a function value, where a and b are parameters of type int. If the number 0 is read, no computation is to be carried out but this 0 is to be delivered as a function value, since it is merely a code to signal the end of the input sequence. Thus $ax + b$ has to be calculated only if x is non-zero, otherwise 0 is the value to be returned. Here is the complete program:

```
main ( )
{ int i, s = 0;
    printf("Enter some integers, followed by 0:\n");
    while (i = read_mul_add(5, 7)) s += i;
    printf("\nThe result is %d\n", s);
}

int read_mul_add(a, b) int a, b;
{ int x;
    scanf("%d", &x);
    return x ? a * x + b : 0;
}
```

We can use this program as follows:

Enter some integers, followed by 0:
2   3   1   0

The result is 51

With the given number sequence the result is computed as:

> $(2 \times 5 + 7) + (3 \times 5 + 7) + (1 \times 5 + 7) = 51$

In this program, *a* and *b* are parameters of function *read_mul_add,* and 5 and 7 are the corresponding arguments. Within the function, $5*x+7$ is actually computed instead of $a*x+b$. A floating-point argument must not be used if the corresponding parameter has integer type, and neither can an integer argument correspond to a floating-point parameter. If we do not specify the types of function value and parameters, and write a function as, for example:

> *read_mul_add(a, b)*
> { ...
> }

type int is assumed, so in our example such omissions are possible. However, it is good programming style to specify the types of function value and parameters, so we prefer:

> *int read_mul_add(a, b) int a, b;*
> { ...
> }

At the point where a function is called, the type of the function value must be known. If that type is not given previously in the program, type int is assumed. To overcome this difficulty, we can specify the type of a function before it is used, in a very simple way. In our example, we can declare:

> *int read_mul_add( );*

either before or after

> *main ( )*
> {

We may omit this declaration, however, because the type is int. In the following program the function *invert* is declared in function *main*:

> *main ( )*
> { *double invert ( );*
>   *printf("%f\n", invert(3));*
> }
>
> *double invert(x) int x;*
> { *return* 1.0/*x*;
> }

If that declaration were omitted, *invert*(3) would be assumed to have an int value, resulting in either a wrong answer or an error message when the type turns out to be double later on.

If our system does not require function *main* to be the first function we can avoid the above additional declaration of *invert* by defining this function before it is called:

> *double invert(x) int x;*
> { *return* 1.0/*x*;
> }

```
main ( )
{ printf("%f\n", invert(3));
}
```

Since not all systems allow this order and since it is more natural to begin with *main*, we prefer the former solution.

Functions need not deliver function values. Here is a program which uses function *pr* to print two given floating-point numbers and their difference in some format:

```
main ( )
{ pr(5.8153, 2.2349); pr(98.2345, 254.3458);
}

pr(x, y) double x, y;
{ printf("7.3f %7.3f    difference: %7.3f\n", x, y, x − y);
}
```

This program has the following output:

```
5.815    2.235    difference:      3.580
98.235   254.346  difference:   −156.111
```

The term *void* is sometimes used for functions such as *pr,* which do not deliver a function value. There are compilers which allow such functions to be declared explicitly, as, for example, in

```
void pr( );
```

In the original version of the C language there was no keyword *void*. In Section 4.6 we shall return to this subject.

If, at some place in a function, immediate return to the calling function is desired the return-statement can be used, even if no value is returned. Thus the following function:

```
f(x, y) int x, y;
{ if (x <y) { printf("x"); return; }
   printf("y");
}
```

is equivalent to

```
f(x, y) int x, y;
{ if (x <y) printf("x"); else printf("y");
}
```

By the way, neither version deserves our admiration, since the following is much more elegant:

```
f(x, y) int x, y;
{ printf(x <y ? "x" : "y");
}
```

Parameters can be used as local variables. If we assign values to them the corresponding arguments will not be affected. The following program illustrates this:

```
main ( )
{ int i = 0;
    p(i); printf("%3d\n", i);
}
p(j) int j;
{ do printf("%3d", ++j); while (j < 5);
}
```

This program prints:

```
    1   2   3   4   5   0
```

The value of variable *i* in function *main* cannot be altered by function *p*. Since only (a copy of) the value of *i* is passed to *p* as an argument, we speak of *call by value*, which is the only parameter-passing mechanism in the C language.

4.2   POINTERS AS PARAMETERS

The restriction to only 'call by value' parameters might seem a serious shortcoming of the C language. However, with pointers as arguments it is no problem to have a function change variables of the calling function. As an example, here is a program which uses a function to exchange the values of two integer variables:

```
main ( )
{ int i = 10, j = 20;
    exchange(&i, &j);
    printf("%2d %2d\n", i, j);
}

exchange(px, py) int *px, *py;
{ int aux;
    aux = *px; *px = *py; *py = aux;
}
```

This program prints the ordered number pair

```
    20   10
```

so the values of *i* and *j* are indeed exchanged. The arguments &*i* and &*j* are the addresses of the variables *i* and *j*. This is reflected by the declaration

```
    int *px, *py;
```

of the parameters. This declaration says *∗px* and *∗py* have type int, so *px* and *py* have type pointer-to-int. In most other languages, instead of *exchange* (&*i*, &*j*) one writes *exchange*(*i*, *j*) to achieve the same goal, and refers to this as *call by reference*, which means that addresses rather than values are passed as arguments. In the C language we write more clearly what we mean, by distinguishing between the notations &*i* and *i*. Although &*i* denotes an address it is, of course, also a value (namely the value of the address, to be distinguished from the value of *i*), so even for a pointer argument such as &*i*, the term 'call by value' is used. Recall that we have already used pointer-arguments in calls of *scanf*, such as in

   scanf("%d", &n)

As a consequence of the close connection between arrays and pointers special rules for array parameters are superfluous.

   In the following program the function *arsum* is called twice. In the first call it is our intention that the entire array *a* is an argument, so that function *arsum* can compute the sum of all array elements. For reasons of generality, the length 100 of the array is supplied as a second argument. The second call is a better demonstration of what function *arsum* actually accomplishes. In this call, the expression $a + 20$ denotes a pointer to element $a[20]$, as if we had written $\&(a[20])$. Counting from this element, the sum of the first 50 elements, that is, $a[20] + a[21] + \ldots + a[69]$, is computed. Similarly, we can understand the first argument *a* in the first call only if we realize that it actually means $\&a[0]$:

```
main ( )
{ int a[100], i, total_sum, partial_sum;
    for (i = 0; i < 100; i++) a[i] = 10 * i;
    total_sum = arsum(a, 100);
    partial_sum = arsum(a + 20, 50);
    printf("%6d %6d\n", total_sum, partial_sum);
}

int arsum(p, n) int *p, n;
{ int s = 0, i;
    for (i = 0; i < n; i++) s += p[i];
    return s;
}
```

The output is:

   49500   22250

In the first line of the function *arsum*, we may replace

   *int *p*

with

   int p[ ]

to express clearly that the argument will be an array. However, both notations are equivalent. The same can be said of the pointer notation $*(p + i)$ that could have been used instead of the array notation $p[i]$ in the above version of *arsum*.

   This example shows that the equivalence of arrays and pointers is quite useful. Functions with array-type parameters also accept pointers which do not point to the first but to some other array element. An application of this principle was shown in Section 3.3, where we used the string-copying function *strcpy*. We are now in a position to discuss how we could define this function ourselves if it were not available as a standard function. If this function definition is fully understood we can write other useful functions, which then can be used as if they were standard functions. A very short version of *strcpy* is

strcpy(*p*, *q*) *char* ∗*p*, ∗*q*;
{ *while* (∗*p*++ = ∗*q*++);
}

To understand this function, we must know that

∗*p*++

ought to be read as

∗(*p*++)

since both ∗ and ++ are unary operators, which associate from right to left. So it is *p* that is incremented (and not ∗*p*). This incrementation takes place after the old value of *p* is used to determine the object that is pointed to. The single equal sign in

∗*p*++ = ∗*q*++

expresses assignation, and should not be confused with the comparison operator ==. Such confusion may easily arise, since in

while (*xxx*)

we expect *xxx* to be a 'logical' expression rather than an assignment. We are therefore inclined to pay attention to the value aspect of *xxx,* rather than to the aspect of action, but both aspects deserve our attention. Repeatedly, ∗*q* is assigned to ∗*p*, and the pointers *p* and *q* are incremented. The character assigned to ∗*p* is also used as the value of the expression, and this value is the null character as soon as the logical end of the string is reached. This null character is equivalent to integer 0, which in a logical context means *false.* So the copying process terminates when the null character has been copied. Note that the while-statement

while (∗*p*++ = ∗*q*++);

also shows a useful application of the null statement, which consists of only a semicolon.

So far, we have used *strcpy* to copy characters from one array to another. The question now arises whether we can use it to shift all characters one or more positions in the same array, such that the old and the new positions overlap. It follows from the order in which the characters are moved that we cannot use *strcpy* to shift right, so

strcpy(*p* + 1, *p*)

is wrong.

If an array has more than one dimension, as discussed in Section 3.4, it can also be passed to a function as an argument. Except for the first one, all dimensions must be specified in the declaration of the formal parameter. For example, let us write a function *printtable,* which prints the lines of a table, along with the sum of the elements of each line. The table may consist of any number of lines, but each line contains precisely five integers. Here is the program:

```
/* TABLEDEMO: This program shows how a table is
                    passed as an argument to a function  */
main ( )
{ int table[3][5], i, j;
  printf("Enter 3 × 5 integers: \n");
  for (i = 0; i < 3; i++)
  for (j = 0; j < 5; j++) scanf("%d", &table[i][j]);
  printtable(table, 3);
}
printtable(a, n) int a[ ][5], n;
{ int s, i, j, num;
  printf("\n%5s %5s %5s %5s %7s\n\n",
     "col. 1", "col. 2, "col. 3", "col. 4", "col. 5", "sum");
  for (i = 0; i < n; i++)
  { s = 0;
    for (j = 0; j < 5; j++)
    { num = a[i][j]; s += num; printf("%5d ", num);
    }
    printf("%7d\n", s);
  }
}
```

In the first line of function *printtable* we could replace

> *int a[ ][5], . . .*

with

> *int a[3][5], . . .*

but not with

> *int a[ ][ ], . . .*

for then the function would not have enough information to compute the address of an element $a[i][j]$. Only if it knows that each row has five columns can it compute the offset $5*i+j$ for the internal position of $a[i][j]$ relative to the start-point of the array.

4.3 PROGRAM PARAMETERS

Like other functions, the function *main* can have parameters. We can pass some strings to our program as we give the command to execute it. If we use the UNIX* operating system we normally type a line consisting only of the program name, which is then the command to execute the program, for example,

> *geometry*

---

* UNIX is a trademark of Bell Laboratories.

if that is the name of the program. Instead, we can type the command line

geometry point line plane . . .

if we wish to provide the program with the four strings *"point"*, *"line"*, *"plane"*, *". . ."*. These strings are used as *program arguments*. The program accepts any number of program arguments, although in the program there are precisely two parameters, conventionally called *argc*, the argument count, and *argv*, the argument vector. For example, we shall use the above command line to execute the following program:

```
main(argc, argv) int argc; char *argv[ ];
{ int i;
    for (i = 0; i < argc; i++) printf("%s\n", argv[i]);
}
```

Then the output of this program is

geometry
point
line
plane
. . .

This example clearly shows the meaning of the program parameters *argc* and *argv*. With the above command line, the first argument *argc* has the value 5, which is equal to the total number of strings in this line, including the program name itself. Each of the first *argc* elements of array *argv* is a pointer to the first character of a null-terminated sequence:

argv[0]	the program name
argv[1]	the first argument
. . .	. . .
argv[*argc* − 1]	the last argument

As the example shows, in the command line the arguments are separated by blanks, and not surrounded by double quotes, though they are internally used as strings. Note that each array element *argv*[*i*] is a pointer to a character, which we are very familiar with, since both the name of a character array and a string constant are also pointers to characters. An array of pointers can be regarded as a pointer to the first array element, which in turn is a pointer. So the name *argv* is in fact a pointer to a pointer, and the first line of the above program can also be written as follows:

main(*argc*, *argv*) *int argc*; *char **argv*;

4.4 IGNORING FUNCTION VALUES

In some languages the distinction between expressions and statements is very essential. We know that in C any expression can be transformed into a statement by placing a semicolon at the end. Although this seems a rather irrelevant language aspect, it has the pleasant consequence that even a function call that returns a value can be turned into a statement by appending a semicolon to it. The returned value is then simply discarded. For example, we can use the following function in two ways:

```
int read_float(p) float *p;
{ scanf("%f", p);
  return *p > 0;
}
```

The function reads a float number, and returns an answer to the question whether this number is positive. This answer is yielded as the function value. As a by-product, the function also delivers that number itself through the pointer parameter p. Now if we only wish to read a number and place it into the location of the float variable x we ignore the function value, and write:

```
read_float(&x);
```

Instead, we can call *read_float* and use its function value, as, for example, in

```
if (read_float(&x)) { /* x > 0 */ ... }
    else { /* x<= 0 */ ...}
```

This aspect of freedom in the way we call functions should not be underestimated. In Section 2.12 we pointed out that, when reading numbers, we can use the value returned by *scanf* to detect some special character that signals the end of the input sequence. As another application, we can use the returned value to cope with invalid input, replacing, for example,

```
scanf("%d", &i);
```

with

```
while (scanf("%d", &i) == 0)
{getchar( ); printf("\nWrong input; enter a number, please: \n");}
```

If now, for example, a letter is entered instead of a number we get a clear message and have another chance. Because of the loop, the program will repeatedly ask for a number until one is entered.

4.5 AUTOMATIC VARIABLES

All variables used so far were declared inside a function, and it makes sense to call them *internal* or *local*. Instead, they are more often referred to as *automatic*, after the fact that their memory space is automatically allocated as the function is entered and released as it is left. In other words, automatic variables are given only temporary memory space. They have no meaning outside the function in which they are declared. The portion of the program where a variable can be used is called the *scope* of that variable. Automatic variables can be declared not only at the beginning of a function but also at the beginning of a compound statement (also called a *block*). Such a compound statement is then the scope of those variables. Parameters of functions, too, have the properties of automatic variables. In the following program the identifier i is used for three distinct variables.

```
main ( )
{ int i = 1; /* This i belongs to function main */
  f(2); printf("i = %2d in function main\n", i);
}

f(i) int i; /* Outermost i in function f */
{ i *= 10;
  /* Here is a compound statement with yet another i: */
  { int i;
    i = 3; printf("i = %2d in innermost block\n", i);
  }
  printf("i = %2d (parameter of function f)\n", i);
}
```

The output is:

```
i =  3 in innermost block
i = 20 (parameter of function f)
i =  1 in function main
```

The variable *i* of *main* is not accessible in function *f*, so its value 1 cannot be altered by that function, as the third output line illustrates. In *f*, parameter *i* is used as a variable. It is multiplied by 10, and its new value 20 is not altered by the innermost compound statement, although the statement

```
i = 3;
```

is executed there. Here we have another variable *i*, declared inside that compound statement, and it is this variable that is given the value 3. When the first closing brace } is reached the memory space for the latter variable *i* is released, and identifier *i* now refers to parameter *i* again. The memory space for this *i* is in turn released as soon as program control returns from *f* to *main*.

Automatic variables have two pleasing aspects. First, memory space is used economically, since it is used only as long as it is needed. Second, their local scope prevents us from affecting them inadvertently in other functions, so variables in other functions need not necessarily be given different names.

For a limited number of variables we can request the compiler to keep them permanently in fast registers. We then add the keyword *register* in their declarations, as, for example, in

```
f(n) register int n;
{ register char ch;
  . . .
}
```

If possible, machine registers, sometimes called accumulators, will now be assigned to the variables *n* and *ch*, which would increase speed. If there are not enough registers available the request will simply be ignored. Only automatic variables and formal parameters are candidates for this facility. Pointers cannot point to them, because pointer values are addresses, and with most machines registers have no addresses.

4.6 EXTERNAL VARIABLES AND PROGRAM STRUCTURE

In the following program, *v* is said to be an *external variable*:

```
int v;
main ( )
{ v = 1; f( );
}

f( )
{ printf("%d\n", v);
}
```

The first line is called the *definition* of *v*. For this variable, permanent memory space is allocated. We can use *v* in both functions *main* and *f*. For external variables the terms 'definition' and 'declaration' are not equivalent. Though not needed in this program, declarations of *v* can be added:

```
int v; /* definition */
main ( )
{ extern int v; /* declaration */
  v = 1; f( );
}

f( )
{ extern int v; /* declaration */
  printf("%d\n", v);
}
```

An external variable has only one definition, and it can have several declarations. Declarations specify attributes of variables. A definition does the same thing, but it also allocates memory space. Roughly speaking, we can say

definition = declaration + memory allocation

In the program text we can easily distinguish these: the declaration of an external variable always begins with the keyword *extern* and a definition does not. In contrast to automatic variables, external variables are defined outside functions.

Large programs usually consist of several modules. Since each module is stored in a file a module is often called a *file*. More specifically, we call them *source files,* to emphasize that they are input files for the compiler. They are compiled separately, and the resulting object files are combined into one executable program by a so-called *linker*, or *linking loader*. This is illustrated in the following diagram:

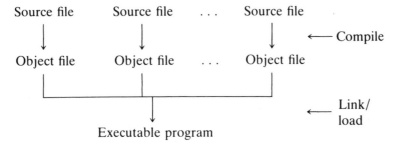

Each source file can contain definitions of external variables and functions. (The program text of a function is said to be the *definition* of that function.) External variables defined in one file can be used in other files, provided that the latter contain declarations of those variables. So in this case declarations of external variables are essential. A declaration inside a function has significance only for that function. If a variable is declared outside a function it is 'visible' from the point of declaration to the end of the file.

In the following example, we have three source files, *A, B* and *C*. Each function is represented by only one line:

File *A*:
main( ) { ... }
extern int v[ ];
*f*1( ) { ... }
*f*2( ) { ... }

File *B*:
*f*3( ) { ... }
int v[100];
*f*4( ) { ... }

File *C*:
*f*5( ) { *extern int v*[ ]; ... }
*f*6( ) { ... }

External array *v* is defined in file *B*, and it is declared in files *A* and *C*. In the definition the array dimension 100 is included so that memory space for variable *v* can be allocated. In the declarations this can be omitted. Here it is only the type that matter. Incidentally, instead of

extern int v[ ];

we could have written

*extern int *v*;

since the name of an array is a pointer to its first element. In file *C*, array *v* is declared inside function *f*5. It is therefore unknown in function *f*6. In file *A*, array *v* is declared outside the functions *main, f*1 and *f*2. Since functions *f*1 and *f*2 are defined after the declaration of array *v*, this array can be used in these functions. It cannot be used in function *main*, because this function precedes the array declaration. Similarly, in file *B* array *v* can be used in *f*4 but not in *f*3.

Functions are always external, so we cannot define a function *f* inside a function *g*. Besides a definition (that is, the function itself) we have to write a declaration for a function if it is used before it is defined, and if, at the same time, it returns a non-integer value. Thus a function needs no separate declaration if it returns either an int value or no value at all, or if, in the same file, it is defined before it is used. As all functions are external, the keyword *extern* in function declarations would give no new information, and can therefore be omitted. Here is an example which illustrates these rules:

    File *A*:
    main( )
    { *int j*;
       *double f*1( ), *a, b, c, d, e*;

       . . .

       *d = f*1(*a*); *j = f*2(*b, c*); *f*3(*j, d, e*);
    }
    *double f*1(*x*) *int x*; { . . . }
    *int f*2(*x, y*) *float x, y*; { . . . }

    File *B*:
    *double f*1( );
    *f*3(*i, x, y*) *int i*; *double x, y*;
    { . . . *y = f*1(*p*); *f*2(*q, r*); . . .
    }
    g( ) { . . . *f*1(123) . . . }

Function *f*1 delivers a value of type double. In file *A* it must be declared since otherwise type int would be assumed when *f*1 is called in *main*. This is why *main* contains the declaration

    *double f*1( ), . . .

In file *B* the same function is declared at the beginning of the file, so that it can be used in both functions *f*3 and *g*. This example demonstrates that in many situations function declarations can be omitted. In file *A* function *f*2 may be used before it is defined, because it has an int function value. Function *f*3 delivers no value at all, and need not be declared either, even though it is defined in another file. In the same way, function *f*2 is used in file *B* although it is not declared there. This is permitted because of its int type. Note that a function declaration specifies information only about the function value, not about the arguments.

Some people consider it good programming style to declare all relevant functions that are defined in other files. In our example, the declaration

    *void f*3( );

may be included in file *A*, and

    *int f*2( );

in file *B*. The keyword *void* was not included in the original version of C but added later, to be used for functions which do not return a value. Should the compiler not understand this new keyword then it can be defined, using

    #*define void int*

if this programming style is preferred.

4.7 STATIC VARIABLES

Variable definitions can be prefixed by the keyword *static*. Let us distinguish between *internal* and *external* static.

Internal static variables are declared (and at the same time defined) inside a function. In contrast to automatic variables, they have permanent memory space. In the following program, *s* is an internal static variable:

```
    main( )
    { int i;
        for (i = 1; i<= 5; i++) printf("%3d %3d\n", i, f(i));
    }
    f(x) int x;
    { static int s = 100;
        return s += x;
    }
```

Since *s* has permanent memory space it keeps the same value in the period of time between leaving function *f* and again entering it later. In contrast to automatic variables, static variables are initialized only once, so here *s* has the value 100 only the first time the function *f* is entered. The output of this program will be as follows:

```
    1   101
    2   103
    3   106
    4   110
    5   115
```

If we had omitted the keyword *static* in the program, *s* would have been initialized to 100 each time the function is entered. Then the output would have been:

```
    1   101
    2   102
    3   103
    4   104
    5   105
```

Initialization, if specified, is always performed at the time that memory is allocated. For an automatic variable this happens on entering the function to which the variable belongs, but static variables are given their space and their initial values at the beginning (or even before) program-execution. If not initialized explicitly, all variables with permanent memory space are initially set to zero.

We may initialize *arrays* only if they have permanent memory space, that is, if they are static or external. If some or all elements of those arrays are not explicitly initialized they are given the default initial values zero. For example, after

```
    static int a[3] = {10, 20}, b[3];
```

the elements of arrays *a* and *b* have the following values:

$a[0] = 10, \ a[1] = 20, \ a[2] = b[0] = b[1] = b[2] = 0$

Here is an example which shows how a two-dimensional array can be initialized:

static double x[2][3] = {{5, 8.2, 7.1}, {3, 4, 5}};

This example also illustrates that, as in assignments, conversions from one type to another will be carried out, if necessary, so the number 5 in this example need not be written as 5.0. If we initialize an array we may omit its first dimension, which is then determined by the number of initial values. Thus our last example may be replaced with:

static double x[ ][3] = {{5, 8.2, 7.1}, {3, 4, 5}};

A convenient notation is available to initialize an array of characters. For example, instead of

static char str[10] = {'A', 'B', 'C'};

we can write

static char str[10] = "ABC";

In both cases the final seven elements of *str* are implicitly initialized to zero, so, as usual, there will be a terminating null character in the array.

Permanent memory space is also assigned to external variables, so we might wonder why we should ever want internal static variables. However, as observed in Section 4.5, it is sometimes an advantage for the scope of a variable to be limited to the function where it is defined. In this way the variable cannot be changed in other functions. Therefore, outside its scope we can use the name of that variable for other purposes, which is convenient, especially in large programs with a great many functions and variables. External variables can be regarded as public property. Internal static variables, on the other hand, are the private property of the function they belong to.

External static variables can be regarded as the private property of the file where they are defined. In other files, access to them is impossible, so declaring them there with the keyword *extern* does not work. Again this might seem to be an unpleasant restriction, but there are positive aspects similar to those mentioned for *internal* static variables. If a variable is not accessible in other files there is no danger that we would inadvertently change it in those files. Not only a variable but also a function can be made local to a file. Function are always external, but often they need be used in only one file. Possible name conflicts can then be avoided by using the keyword *static*. This is especially relevant with respect to system functions whose names we wish to use for other purposes. An example is the name *open*, which is a standard function in many C implementations. Suppose that either we do not know this or we insist on using the same name for a function of our own. We can then add the keyword *static*, as in the following example, which also shows the definition of the external static variable *v*. The definition of the variable *v* and the functions *main* and *open* occur in the same file:

```
static int v;
main( )
{ ... open(a, b); ...
}
static open(x, y) int x, y;
{ ...
}
```

The keyword *static* prevents other files from having access to the variable *v* and to the function *open* defined in this file. Moreover, if we make indirect use of a system function also called *open* no confusion can arise. (The term 'indirect' refers to the possibility that we should use some standard function which in turn uses the system function *open*.)

4.8 PREPROCESSOR FACILITIES

Our programs may contain lines beginning with the character **#**, and known as *compiler control lines*. Such program lines cause the programs to be modified before they are compiled. For example, the program

```
#define LEN 100
main( )
{ printf("%d\n", LEN * LEN);
}
```

is internally replaced with the following program

```
main( )
{ printf("%d\n", 100 * 100);
}
```

and subsequently compiled. Each occurrence of the identifier *LEN* as a token is replaced with the string 100 that follows this identifier in the #*define* line. This means that *LEN* is not replaced with 100 if it is part of a longer identifier, such as *LENGTH*. Note that the string that is used starts at the position after the white space following the identifier, and ends at the end of the line.

We can also use #*define* lines with parameters. We begin with a very simple but yet interesting example. In the first line of the following program a so-called *macro* is defined, whose name is *max*:

```
#define max(x, y) x > y ? x : y
main( )
{ int i, j;
  float a, b;
  printf("Enter two integers and two real numbers: ");
  scanf("%d %d %f %f", &i, &j, &a, &b);
  printf("\nMaximum values: %d %f\n", max(i, j), max(a, b));
}
```

In this example, the string

$i > j ? i : j$

replaces $max(i, j)$, and the string

$a > b ? a : b$

replaces $max(a, b)$. Thus $max(i, j)$ and $max(a, b)$ are not function calls, although they have the same syntax. Note, however, that the program does not work if we remove the #*define* line and add the function

float max(x, y) float x, y; {return(x > y ? x : y);}

For the call $max(a, b)$, the function type should indeed be float, but for $max(i, j)$ it should be int. The problem is that we cannot write a function whose type depends on the arguments, so we should need two distinct functions, say *max* for integer and *fmax* for floating-point values. With macros we have no such problems. In practice, we do not define a macro *max* in the way shown above but rather as follows:

#*define max(x, y) ((x) > (y) ? (x) : (y))*

In this way, we can also use the macro in more complicated contexts, such as

$a = 1 + max(b = c + 2, d);$

In this example it is our intention to assign the value of $c + 2$ to b, and to compare this value with d. One plus the larger of these two values is then to be assigned to a. The macro expansion for this line becomes

$a = 1 + ((b = c + 2) > (d) ? (b = c + 2) : (d));$

This is not exactly an example of efficiency, since $b = c + 2$, if larger than d, is executed twice, but at least it gives the correct result, which would not have been the case if we had used our previous definition of *max*. Without the extra parentheses the expansion would have read

$a = 1 + b = c + 2 > d ? b = c + 2 : d;$

which is incorrect. In general it is a good idea to use a good many parentheses in macro definitions. It is also worth remembering that in

#*define max(. . .*

no space may appear between the name *max* and the first parenthesis, since otherwise the macro definition would be interpreted as our first and very simple version, where we had no parameters. For example, with

#*define max (x, y) ((x) > (y) ? (x) : (y))*

the blank following the identifier *max* has the very undesirable effect that when we use this macro, *max* will be replaced with

$(x, y)((x) > (y) > (y) ? (x) : (y))$

which does not make sense.

As in strings, we can use the backslash to continue the line that defines a macro, so that logically a #*define* line can be as long as we wish.

Scope rules for macros are different from those for proper program-identifiers. A macro is in effect from its definition to either the end of the file or a line of the form

> #*undef macro-name*

Here is an example:

```
int N = 100; /* external variable */
main( )
{ printf("%d\n", N); /* 100 */
  #define N 123
  printf("%d\n", N); /* 123 */
  f( );
}

f( )
{ printf("%d\n", N); /* 123 */
  #undef N
  printf("%d\n", N); /* 100 */
}
```

This program prints the numbers 100, 123, 123, 100 in that order, so the named constant $N = 123$ is in effect between the #*define* and the #*undef* line, although these preprocessor lines occur in distinct functions.

We can include the contents of a file by writing a line of the form

> #*include "filename"*

or

> #*include ⟨filename⟩*

This preprocessor line is replaced with the contents of the file with the given file name. For standard files, such as *stdio. h,* we use the form ⟨*filename*⟩. Our own directory is first searched for the given file name if the form *"filename"* with double quotes is used. If not found there, the 'standard' directory is searched, as if the form ⟨*filename*⟩ were used. In practice include-files often contain #*define*-lines.

Conditional compilation of some portion of the program is realized by

> #*if constant-expression*
>
> . . .
>
> #*else*
>
> . . .
>
> #*endif*

The constant-expression must not contain variables or function calls. It is evaluated during compilation. If its value is non-zero, the first program portion indicated by . . . is compiled. As in a normal if-statement, the #*else*-part is optional. If present, the program fragment . . . between #*else* and #*endif* is compiled only if the constant-expression has the value 0. Instead of

> #if *constant-expression*

we can use

> #ifdef *identifier*

if it is desired to test whether an identifier has been defined by means of a
#define-line. Similarly, we can use

> #ifndef *identifier*

which means 'if *identifier* is not defined . . .'. In very simple programs consisting of
only one file we feel no need for conditional compilation. Here is an example where
two files are involved:

```
File A. H:
  #define N 1000
File B. C:
  #include "A. H"
  main( )
  {
  #ifndef N
    printf("#define-line for N missing in file A. H\n");
  #else
    #if N <= 100
      float matrix[N][N];
      . . . /* rest of program */
    #else
      printf("Matrix needs too much memory: N too large\n");
    #endif
  #endif
  }
```

With the above contents of file *A. H*, compilation of file *B. C* causes the message

> *Matrix needs too much memory*: *N too large*

to be printed. (The portion between the #if and the #else line is completely
ignored, so although syntactically incorrect due to the three dots . . . , the above
version can be used literally!)

Finally, there are compiler control lines of the form

> #line *constant identifier*

as, for example,

> #line 1000 *ABC*

If the compiler produces a listing with line numbers it will now assign the numbers
1000, 1001, . . . to the program lines that follow. At the same time the compiler will
now use the name *ABC* instead of the name of the current input file if such a name
is to be included in the program listing. The identifier may be absent, as, for

example, in

  #*line* 1000

In this case the remembered file name does not change.

4.9 STANDARD FUNCTIONS

In Section 2.12 we discussed several standard functions for input and output, and in Chapter 6 some more will follow. Here we shall discuss some other standard functions, mainly those which have to do with mathematics and those for character-handling. Instead of 'standard functions' we also call them 'library functions', 'built-in functions' or 'predefined functions'. As the term 'library function' indicates, there are a great many of them, and actually they are not part of the language, so, strictly speaking, a C textbook can omit them and refer to the manufacturer's manuals. On the other hand, as soon as we write a C program we need these functions, and it is very convenient to have a list of them available in a book like this. This list should be shorter and more informal than an authoritative document such as, for example, the UNIX *User's Manual*. The functions mentioned here are only a subset of those which we can use on our machine. Those selected here are widely available and particularly useful. Most of them are therefore worth remembering.

When using standard functions we often include so-called *header files*. For example, the standard header file *math. h* is included in our program (usually at the beginning) by writing:

  #*include* ⟨*math. h*⟩

This header file contains function declarations such as

  double sin( ), *cos*( ), . . .

so it relieves us from the obligation to include these declarations explicitly. Recall that any function with a non-integer function value must be declared before it is used. Instead of these declarations we shall use a notation which also gives information about the arguments that are expected. In fact this notation can be regarded as the first line of the function definition. Remember that these lines will not actually occur in our programs but are only a formal notation to discuss the returned value and the arguments. These lines are often referred to as a *synopsis* of the function under consideration. Each synopsis is accompanied by a brief comment that indicates what the function computes. After the line #*include* ⟨*math. h*⟩ we can use the functions listed below:

double cos(x) *double x*;	/* *cos x*	*/
double sin(x) *double x*;	/* *sin x*	*/
double tan(x) *double x*;	/* *tan x*	*/
double exp(x) *double x*;	/* *exp x*	*/
double log(x) *double x*;	/* *ln x*	*/
double log 10(x) *double x*;	/* 10 *log x*	*/
double pow(x, y) *double x, y*;	/* *x raised to the power y*	*/

double sqrt(x) double x;	*/* the square root of x *|*
double floor(x) double x;	*/* floor(4.9) = 4.0 etc. *|*
double ceil(x) double x;	*/* ceil(4.9) = 5.0 etc. *|*
int abs(i) int i;	*/* integer absolute value *|*
double fabs(x) double x;	*/* floating absolute value *|*
double acos(x) double x;	*/* arccos x *|*
double asin(x) double x;	*/* arcsin x *|*
double atan(x) double x;	*/* arctan x *|*
double cosh(x) double x;	*/* cosh x *|*
double sinh(x) double x;	*/* sinh x *|*
double tanh(x) double x;	*/* tanh x *|*
int atoi(str) char *str;	*/* atoi("12345") = 12345 etc. *|*
double atof(str) char * str;	*/* atof("12.3E − 1") = 1.23 *|*

Whenever angles are involved they are expressed in radians, not in degrees. As the comments illustrate, the last two functions convert strings to the appropriate numeric values. Of course, this works properly only if the given string contains a sequence of characters representing a number. The above list contains two functions which do not really require the include file *math. h,* namely *abs* and *atoi,* since they yield an int value.

We shall now deal with some functions for character-handling. The function *strcpy* to copy strings was discussed in Sections 3.3 and 4.2. However, we ignored its function value, which is simply equal to its first argument. In many cases we feel no need to use this function value, and then we can use the function without declaring it, as we did in Section 3.3. Should we wish to use the function value, then we have to declare the function as

    char *strcpy( );

Under UNIX, we can instead write

    #include ⟨string. h⟩

since the file *string.h* contains that declaration, among others. This also applies to the functions *strncpy, strcat, strncat.* Since the functions *strcmp, strncmp* and *strlen* yield integer values they need not be declared. Here is some more information about these functions, again in the form of a synopsis and a brief description for each of them:

char *strcpy(p, q) char *p, *q;

    Copies string *q* to *p,* stopping after the null character has been copied. The value *p* is returned.

char *strncpy(p, q, n) char *p, *q; int n;

    Copies exactly *n* characters from *q* to *p.* If *n* characters have been copied without encountering a null character, the result is not null-terminated. If a null character is encountered in position *q + j,* where *j* is less than *n,* the final *n − j* characters of the result are null characters. The value *p* is returned.

char *strcat(p, q) char *p, *q;

Appends a copy of string *q* to the end of string *p*. The valued *p* is returned.

*char *strncat(p, q, n) char *p, *q; int n;*

At most, *n* characters of *q* are copied to the end of *p*. The value *p* is returned.

*int strcmp(p, q) char *p, *q;*

Compares the strings *p* and *q*. If the strings are equal, the function returns 0; if not, it returns a negative integer if *p* is lexicographically less then *p*, and a positive number otherwise.

*int strncmp(p, q, n) char *p, *q; int n;*

Performs the same comparison as *strcmp*, except that now at most *n* characters are compared.

*int strlen(p) char *p;*

Returns the number of characters of string *p*, not including the null character. For example, the value of *strlen("ABC")* is 3.

Because of the similarity in the way we use them we often use the term 'standard functions' for what are actually macros. We shall now discuss some standard macros. Unlike genuine standard functions, for macros the files that define them must be included, regardless of the type of the returned value. A well-known example is *getchar( )*. This is a macro defined in the header file *stdio. h*. Though returning an integer value, *getchar* requires this file to be included, otherwise it would be considered to be a function, and after compilation the linking loader would look for it in vain. Another distinction between macros and functions will be made clear in Section 4.10: we can manipulate pointers to functions, not pointers to macros. We shall now list some macros defined in the header file *ctype. h*. After the line

    #include ⟨ctype. h⟩

we can use the following macros (like functions) to classify characters. The value returned is 1 or 0, depending on whether the question on the same line is answered 'yes' or 'no', respectively. As usual, *ch* has type char:

isalpha(ch)	Is *ch* a letter?
isupper(ch)	Is *ch* an upper-case letter?
islower(ch)	Is *ch* a lower-case letter?
isdigit(ch)	Is *ch* a digit (0–9)?
isxdigit(ch)	Is *ch* a hexadecimal digit (0–9, $A - F$, $a - f$)?
isalnum(ch)	Is *ch* alphanumeric (letter or a digit)?
isspace(ch)	Is *ch* a blank, a tab, or a newline?

The following macros, also defined in *ctype. h*, translate from upper to lower case and vice versa:

tolower(ch)

If *ch* is an upper-case letter, the value returned is the corresponding lower-case letter. Otherwise *ch* is returned.

toupper(*ch*)

If *ch* is a lower-case letter, the value returned is the corresponding upper-case letter. Otherwise *ch* is returned.

In contrast to these macros, here are four genuine functions:

exit(*status*) *int status*;

Terminates the program, closing all open files (see Chapter 6). The argument is returned to the operating system, or, in general, to the program which started our program. Through this argument we can indicate whether the program terminated successfully (*status* = 0) or abnormally (*status* ≠ 0). For example, after an input error is detected, we can print an error message and then quit the program by *exit*(1).

long time(*p*) *long* *p;

Returns the time in seconds elapsed since some fixed moment, for example 1 January 1970, 0.00h GMT. The argument points to the place where the returned time is also stored. See *srand* for a useful application.

srand(*seed*) *int seed*;

If we want to use the function *rand* to generate pseudo-random numbers we first call *srand* (usually only once) with some integer which is the seed of the random-number generator. If the random numbers are to be different each time our program is run, we can use the function *time* to obtain a truly pseudo-random seed value. For example:

```
long *p;
. . .
time(p); srand((int)*p);
```

int rand( )

Returns a pseudo-random number in the form of a (large) integer. We usually apply the remainder operator % to the returned value. For example, a random number in the range $0, 1, \ldots, 99$ is obtained by computing

```
rand( ) % 100
```

A seed value for the random-number generator can be specified by a call of *srand*.

More standard functions are dealt with elsewhere in this book, namely:
(1) *malloc, realloc, free* (in Section 5.3) and
(2) Functions for I/O (in Section 2.12 and Chapter 6).

4.10 POINTERS TO FUNCTIONS

This section deals with a language aspect which will be appreciated by the more advanced users of C. As it concerns functions, it belongs in this chapter, but if the reader finds it difficult he can skip it and return to it later.

Functions are stored in memory in much the same way as data. Reflecting on this, we should not be surprised that functions, too, have addresses that can be assigned to pointers. Although this is essentially simple, the notation for those pointers is somewhat cryptic in that we have to be extremely careful with parentheses and the unary operator *. If p is a pointer to a function that has no parameters, a call of that function can be written as

   $(*p)( )$

The parentheses in $(*p)$ cannot be omitted, since in

   $*f( )$

the parentheses have higher precedence than *, so the latter form is read as

   $*(f( ))$

which denotes the object pointed to by the value returned by f. Thus f is a function returning a pointer. The parentheses surrounding $*p$, not $*f$, also occur in the declarations, for example:

   int $(*p)( )$;   /* *p is a pointer to a function*   */
   int $*f( )$;   /* *f is a function returning a pointer* */

Functions like f, yielding a pointer, are quite common. An example is *strcpy* in Section 4.9. Here we shall restrict ourselves to pointers such as p, pointing to functions. They are relatively rare but nevertheless are worth studying.

Let us assume that at some point in a program we have to decide which of the three functions *cos, sin, tan* has to be used in the rest of the program. We can then establish a pointer to the selected function and subsequently use that pointer. The following program illustrates this:

```
/* PFUNC1: A pointer to a function */
#include <stdio.h>
#include <ctype.h>
#include <math.h>
main( )
{ char ch;
  double (*p)( );
  printf("Enter c, s, or t, to select one\n");
  printf("of the functions cos, sin, tan: ");
  ch = tolower(getchar( ));
  switch(ch)
  { case 'c': p = cos; break;
    case 's': p = sin; break;
    case 't': p = tan; break;
    default : printf("Wrong character\n"); exit(1);
  }
  printf("\n\nArgument     Function value\n");
  printf("%8.3f     %12.8f\n", 0.1, (*p)(0.1));
  printf("%8.3f     %12.8f\n", 0.3, (*p)(0.3));
  printf("%8.3f     %12.8f\n", 1.6, (*p)(1.6));
}
```

Here is a demonstration of this program:

Enter c, s, or t, to select one
of the functions cos, sin, tan: s

Argument	Function value
0.100	0.09983342
0.300	0.29552021
1.600	0.99957360

Note that in an assignment such as

$p = sin;$

the bare function name *sin* is considered to be the address of the function. In the call, however, we write $(*p)$ instead of the function name *sin*, as in

$(*p)(0.1)$

which, after the above assignment, computes $sin(0.1)$.

In other languages functions can be passed as arguments to other functions (or procedures or subroutines). For example, in numerical analysis a general integration routine is called with the interval boundaries and the function to be integrated as arguments. In C we achieve this by means of pointers to functions. Since some of us may not be familiar with numerical analysis we shall use a simpler example.

Let us assume that we want a function *sumfun* which computes the sum

$$s = f(1) + f(1/2) + f(1/3) + \ldots + f(1/n)$$

for any real-valued function f which is defined for those arguments. The function *sumfun* will have both n and a pointer to function f as its arguments. We shall demonstrate this function, choosing $n = 3$ and $f(x) = x^2$ as its arguments:

```
/* PFUNC2: A function as an argument   */
main( )
{ double fun( ), sumfun( );
   printf("Sum: %f\n", sumfun(3, fun));
}
double sumfun(n, f) int n; double (*f)( );
{ double s = 0; int i;
   for (i = 1; i<= n; i++) s += (*f)(1.0/i);
   return s;
}
double fun(x) double x;
{ return x*x;
}
```

This program computes

$$1 + \frac{1}{4} + \frac{1}{9}$$

so its output is

Sum: 1.361111

Pointers to functions can be placed in an array. This is illustrated by the following program, which prints the values of *cos*(1.0), *sin*(1.0) and *tan*(1.0):

```
/* PFUNC3: Array of pointers to functions */
#include ⟨math. h⟩
main( )
{ int i;
    double (*a[3])( );
    a[0] = cos;
    a[1] = sin;
    a[2] = tan;
    for (i = 0; i < 3; i++) printf("%10.7f\n", (*a[i])(1.0));
}
```

Here is the output of this program:

```
0.5403023
0.8414710
1.5574077
```

No doubt, in this program the line

$$double\ (*a[3])(\ );$$

is the most difficult one, especially if we have to invent it ourselves. It consists of the following three components:
(1) A type-specifier: *double*
(2) A declarator: $(*a[3])(\ )$
(3) A semicolon: ;

Since the declarator is the most difficult component we will pay some attention to it. An identifier (here the letter *a*) is the simplest form of a declarator. Once we have a declarator, the following forms are also declarators:

declarator [constant-expression]
*declarator
(declarator)
declarator( )

Successive application of these formation rules to the array name *a* leads to the complex declarator of our example. The formation rules may be used in any order, but here we have used the order indicated above. The declarator we need can also be derived from the expression

$$(*a[i])(1.0)$$

occurring in the program (second line from bottom). To obtain the desired declarator all we have to do is replace the subscript *i* by the array dimension 3 and remove the function argument 1.0. Note how the precedence rules of Section 2.7 are applied to the three operators *, [ ], ( ). Since [ ] have higher precedence than *, the array element *a[i]* itself need not be surrounded by parentheses. On the other hand, the parentheses in (*a[i]) cannot be omitted, for the operator ( ) following it also has higher precedence than *.

Another complex declarator will appear if we wish to define a function which returns a pointer to another function. Here is a program which contains such a function:

```
/* PFUNC4: A function returning a function!  */
#include ⟨math. h⟩
main( )
{ double (*fun( ))( );
  printf("sin(1.0) = %9.7f\n", (*fun('s'))(1.0));
}

double (*fun(ch))( ) char ch;
{ switch(ch)
  { case 'c': return cos; break;
    case 's': return sin; break;
    case 't': return tan; break;
  }
}
```

This program has the following output:

$$sin(1.0) = 0.8414710$$

To understand the rather complicated notations in this program, we begin with studying the actual function call

$$(*fun('s'))(1.0)$$

Remember that $*fun('s')$ is the object pointed to by the pointer $fun('s')$ returned by the call of *fun*. That object is the *sin* function, which is supplied with the argument 1.0. Again we remove the arguments to obtain the declarator occurring in the declaration of *fun* at the beginning of *main*. In the definition of *fun* (the function itself) the formal parameter *ch* is written in the same position as the corresponding argument $'s'$ in the function call.

4.11 EXAMPLES

Example 1

Write a function to compute *n*-factorial ($=n!$).

SOLUTION (including a main program)

```
main( )
{ double nfact( );
  printf("%f\n", nfact(3));
}
double nfact(n) int n;
{ int i;
  double x = 1.0;
  for (i = 2; i<= n; i++) x *= i;
  return x;
}
```

Example 2

Use Euclid's algorithm to compute the Greatest Common Divisor (*gcd*) of two integers. According to that algorithm, the *gcd* of *a* and *b* is found as the *gcd* of *b* and *r*, where *r* is the remainder of *a* divided by *b*. This rule applies only if *b* is non-zero, otherwise we simply use *gcd*(*a*, 0) = *a*. For example, we have:

$$gcd(2048, 224) = gcd(224, 32) = gcd(32, 0) = 32$$

The function *gcd* can be written very briefly:

```
int gcd(a, b) int a, b;
{ return (b ? gcd(b, a % b) : a);
}
```

(Instead of *b* ? . . . you may read *b* != 0 ? . . .)

This is our first example of a recursive function. It calls itself, which is very natural in this case since the above formulation of Euclid's algorithm expresses the *gcd* in terms of itself. Note that the function also works properly if *a* is less then *b*, since then *a* is the resulting remainder, so we have, for example,

$$gcd(224, 2048) = gcd(2048, 224) = . . .$$

Example 3

We want a function which sorts an integer array. The array elements are to be placed in ascending order. We will use a well-known method called *Quicksort* (C. A. R. Hoare, *Computer Journal*, April 1962). This method is based on partitioning the given sequence into two subsequences such that each element of the first sequence is not greater than a certain value (*x* in our function *qsort*) and each element of the second subsequence is not less than that value. Then the function (*qsort*) is recursively applied to both subsequences, and so on. Since we want to apply *qsort* to any subsequence, we shall use the two extreme left and right boundaries of the subsequence as arguments. Here is a complete program, which includes the desired function *qsort*:

```
/* SORT: A demonstration of Quicksort using pointers  */
#define MAX 5000
main( )
{ int a[MAX], n = 0, i, x;
    printf("Enter (at most %d) integers, \n", MAX);
    printf("the last one followed by #:\n");
    while (n < MAX && scanf("%d", &x)) a[n++] = x;
    /* scanf returns 0 if # is read instead of a number  */
    qsort(a, a + n - 1);
    printf("\n\nSorted numbers:\n"); /* five on a line  */
    for (i = 0; i < n; i++ )
        printf("%c%9d", i % 5 ? ' ' : '\n', a[i]);
    printf("\n");
}
```

```
qsort(left, right) int *left, *right;
{ int *p = left, *q = right, x = *(left + (right − left)/2), w;
  do
  { while ( *p < x ) p++;
    while ( *q > x ) q−−;
    if (p > q) break;
    w = *p; *p = *q; *q = w;
  } while ( ++p <= −−q);
  if (left < q) qsort(left, q);
  if (p < right) qsort(p, right);
}
```

Here is a demonstration of this program:

Enter (at most 5000) integers,
the last one followed by #:

935	111	299	234	123
−12	0	1	100	111
123	999	472	23	−1
#				

Sorted numbers:

−12	−1	0	1	23
100	111	111	123	123
234	299	472	935	999

The arguments of *qsort* are pointers. Instead, we could have used array subscript values, but then the name of the array should also have been made available to *qsort*. Then either an additional (array) argument or an externally defined array would have been required. Since the former is less efficient and the latter less elegant, we prefer the above solution with pointers.

4.12 EXERCISES

4.1   What will be printed by the following program?

```
int i = 8;
main( )
{ int i = 10, *p;
  p = &i;
  (*p)++;
  printf("Result A: %2d\n", i);
  ppp(i);
  printf("Result B: %2d\n", i);
}

ppp(j) int j;
{ j++;
  printf("Result C: %2d\nResult D: %2d\n", i, j);
}
```

4.2   Write a function which reads a floating-point number, skipping over any preceding non-numeric characters.

4.3   Write the function *rectangle* (l, w) which prints a rectangle whose sides consist of asterisks. The length and the width of the rectangle are l and w, respectively. For example, if $l = 10$ and $w = 4$, the following rectangle is printed:

```
**********
*        *
*        *
**********
```

4.4   Write the function *order*4, such that, for int variables a, b, c, d, the call

  *order*4(&a, &b, &c, &d)

takes care that

  $a \leqslant b \leqslant c \leqslant d$

by interchanging the values of these variables.

4.5   Write a program which reads a positive integer n and prints all permutations of the numbers $1, 2, \ldots, n$. For example, if $n = 3$, we can have the following output:

  1 2 3   1 3 2   2 1 3   2 3 1   3 1 2   3 2 1

Hint:

This problem can best be solved by means of a recursive function *perm* and an external array a. Initially, we set $a[1] = 1$, $a[2] = 2, \ldots, a[n] = n$. Then, for $k > 0$, any call *perm*(k) successively interchanges $a[k]$ with each of the preceding array elements, recursively calling *perm*($k - 1$) each time. Every call *perm*(0) prints the contents of $a[1]$, $a[2], \ldots, a[n]$. The main program contains the call *perm*(n).

4.6   Write a program which reads n and k, and prints all combinations of k distinct elements selected from the numbers $1, 2, \ldots, n$. As in Exercise 4.5, this problem can be solved by means of a recursive function with a single integer argument related to the recursion depth.

CHAPTER 5

Structures and dynamic memory-allocation

5.1 INTRODUCTION

It is sometimes convenient to regard a collection of variables as a single object. Suppose that we are developing an information system for people, where each person's name, year of birth and length are the relevant data items. In C we can combine these data items into a so-called *structure*:

name	year	length
J.Smith	1970	185

If a structure of this type has the name *S,* its members are denoted by

$S.\ name,\quad S.\ year,\quad S.\ length$

Let us assume that a person's name consists of, at most, 30 characters (so 31 positions will be necessary to include the null character at the end) and that both the year of birth and the length (in cm) are integers. In the following declaration we introduce *S* and *T* as variables of this structure type. Besides, *people* is an array consisting of 100 such variables:

    struct { char name[31]; *int year, length;* } *S, T, people*[100];

This line is essentially of the same form as

    int i, j, a[100];

so

    struct { char name[31]; *int year, length;* }

is a (non-elementary) data type, comparable with *int.* We can insert a *tag* immediately after the keyword *struct.* In this way we can abbreviate the type notation to provide for a shorter notation in case we need it later. This is shown in the following example, which can be used instead of the above declaration of *S, T,* and *people*:

    struct person
    { *char name*[31];
      int year, length;
    } *S, T;*
    struct person people[100];

We see that *struct person* is now the abbreviated notation for our structure type.

This example also shows the way in which complicated structured types are usually written on several lines. Some C-users will even use one line more, and replace

int year, length;

with

int year;
int length;

Another equivalent way to declare *S, T,* and *people* is:

struct person { char name[31]; *int year, length*; };
struct person S, T, people[100];

Note that in the last line the keyword *struct* must not be omitted. If we wish to get rid of this obligation we can use another way of introducing a new identifier to denote a data type. Beginning with a simple example, we can write

typedef double REAL;

After this definition of *REAL* (which is not a keyword) this identifier can be used instead of the keyword *double,* as, for example, in

REAL x, a[100];

In general, a typedef declaration has the form

typedef 'known type' 'new identifier';

Reverting to our structure type, we can finally declare *S, T,* and *people* as follows:

typedef struct { char name[31]; *int year, length*; } *PERSON*;
PERSON S, T, people[100];

In each of the above declarations, the variables can be initialized, provided their memory space is permanent. (As discussed in Chapter 4, the latter means that these variables can only be initialized if they are external or static). For example, we can write

static PERSON
  S = { *"J. Smith"*, 1970, 185 },
  T,
  people[100] =
    {{ *"H. Adams"*, 1961, 168 },
    { *"P. Collins"*, 1965, 170 }
    };

In this case the variables *S, people*[0], *people*[1] are given appropriate initial values.

Having paid so much attention to the various ways in which structures can be declared we now want to use them. We can copy the entire contents of *S* to *T* by the assignment statement

T = S;

The older C compilers did not allow this. Instead, we had to copy the structure members one by one, which, of course, is still valid (and even necessary if only some members are to be copied):

strcpy(T. name, S. name);
T. year = S. year;
T. length = S. length;

We also need the individual members if a structure is to be printed. For example:

printf("%−30s %4d %3d\n", S. name, S. year, S. length);

(The format item %−30s causes a string to be left-adjusted, that is, padded on the right with blanks, in a field of 30 positions.)

We frequently use pointers to structures, especially in connection with functions and arrays. Let us assume that the *i*th element of array *people* is to be used. Conventionally, we denote its members as follows

people[i]. name
people[i]. year
people[i]. length

and the *j*th character of the first of these three members is

people[i]. name[j]

(Since the dot and the array brackets are operators with the same precedence, and since they associate from left to right, the latter construct should be read as

((people[i]). name)[j]

which form, incidentally, could be used literally!). We see that the operation of subscripting to have access to *people[i]* will be carried out quite often. In such cases we can improve efficiency by using a pointer to people[i]. If we declare

*struct person *ptr;*

the assignment statement

ptr = people + i;

enables us to have access to *people[i]. length,* for example, by using the notation

*(*ptr). length*

Here the parentheses cannot be omitted, since the dot has higher precedence than the asterisk. There is, however, a special notation for this case, where we select a member of a structure to which a pointer is given. The two characters −>, to be read as one operator, are written between the pointer and the member name, so in our example we can write

ptr −> length

Similarly, the other members of *people[i]* can now be written

ptr −> year   and   *ptr −> name*

The individual characters of the latter member are

   $ptr -> name [j]$ $(j = 0, 1, \ldots, 30)$

where again the operators $->$ and [ ] have the same precedence and associate from left to right.

As this example shows, structures can have arrays as their members and, conversely, elements of arrays can be structures. Similarly, a member of a structure can in turn be a structure, so there is no restriction in respect of the complexity of data types.

We shall use structures in the following sections, some of which deal with rather advanced topics. If the reader prefers dealing with files as soon as possible, he can postpone studying these remaining sections and skip to Chapter 6. Some elementary knowledge of structures will be required there, since any access to a file will be through a file pointer, which is in fact a pointer to a structure.

5.2 FUNCTIONS AND STRUCTURES

We shall now study a complete program. This shows how structures are used and, in particular, how a pointer to a structure is passed as an argument to a function. The program is part of an information system, mentioned at the beginning of this chapter, and deals with names, years of birth and lengths. The program first reads such data from the keyboard for, at most, 100 people. Then another year of birth can be entered, with the effect of printing the data of all people who have at least the age that corresponds to that year of birth. The latter process can be repeated several times, so once the complete list of personal data is entered, several lists of people with some minimum age can be produced. Only the first 30 positions of a name will be stored, and each name is immediately followed by a semicolon. After the last person an exclamation mark at the beginning of a new line signals the end of the first part of the input data. When we have obtained all the lists we want, the word *END* can be used to stop program-execution. Here is the complete program:

```
/* VITAL
 Very Interesting Tables concerning Ages and Lengths */
#include <stdio. h>
#define TABLE_LENGTH 100
#define NAME_LENGTH 30
struct person
{ char name[NAME_LENGTH + 1];
  int year, length;
};

main( )
{ char ch;
  struct person people[TABLE_LENGTH + 1], *p;
  int latest_year, i, n = 0;
  printf("Enter a line with personal data, for example: ");
  printf("John Smith; 1970 185\n");
  while (n < TABLE_LENGTH && (ch = getchar( ), ch != '!'))
```

```
      { ungetc(ch, stdin);
        p = people + n++;
        readname(p);
        scanf("%d %d", &(p -> year), &(p -> length));
        printf("Another one (or !), please: \n");
        do ; while (getchar( ) != '\n'); /* skip to next line */
      }
      while (
        printf("\nEnter a year of birth, or END to stop: "),
        scanf("%d", &latest_year) > 0)
      { printf("\nPeople of the corresponding age or older: \n\n");
        for (i = 0; i < n; i++)
        { p = people + i;
            if (p -> year <= latest_year)
              printf("%-30s %4d %3d\n",
                      p -> name, p -> year, p -> length);
        }
      }
    }

    readname(ptr) struct person *ptr;
    { int j = 0;
      char ch;
      while (ch = getchar( ), ch != ';')
      if (j < NAME_LENGTH) ptr -> name[j++] = ch;
      ptr -> name[j] = '\0';
    }
```

Here is a demonstration of how program VITAL can be used:

Enter a line with personal data, for example: John Smith; 1970 185
Peter MacArthur; 1950 180
Another one (or !), please:
Leonardo Marcelli Mario del Gallardo; 1940 155
Another one (or !), please:
Bob Nickleby; 1962 165
Another one (or !), please:
Mary Stewart; 1970 160
Another one (or !), please:
Pamela Johnson; 1963 170
Another one (or !), please:
!

Enter a year of birth, or END to stop: 1962

People of the corresponding age or older:

Peter MacArthur   1950 180
Leonardo Marcelli Mario del Ga 1940 155
Bob Nickleby   1962 165
Enter a year of birth, or END to stop: END

In the first loop the assignment statement

$p = people + n++;$

should be interpreted as

$p = \&(people[n]); n = n + 1;$

The pointer value p is passed to function *readname* so that characters can be placed into the name member of the proper element of array *people*. Note that the name *people* itself is not known inside function *readname*, since it is declared inside function *main*. The tag *person*, however, is declared at the global level, outside function *main*, so that we can use it in the line

   *readname(ptr) struct person *ptr;*

In the function *readname* characters are read until a semicolon is encountered. If the maximum name length is exceeded (as with the long Italian name in the example), there is a provision to prevent array-overflow. Although all characters of the name are read, only the first 30 are stored into the positions $0, 1, \ldots, 29$. A null character is placed at the end.

   Function *readname* can be called before it is declared, because it does not return a value whose type has to be known. Its argument is a pointer to a structure. Now suppose that we need a function which returns such a pointer as its function value. Let us, for example, write the function *find*, such that the call in

   $p = find(people, n, len);$

returns a pointer to the first structure in array *people* of which the length member has the value *len*, if there is such a structure. If there is none, the function will return the null pointer *NULL*, defined in the header file *stdio. h* as

   #define NULL 0

Since this function returns a non-integer value, we have to declare it in the following way before we can use it:

   *struct person *find( );*

We can insert this line either in or before the function where *find* is called. The function *find* itself, that is to say its definition, can be placed at the end of the program in the following form:

```
struct person *find(p, np, leng)
   struct person *p; int np, leng;
{ int i;
   for (i = 0; i < np; i++)
     if (p[i]. length == leng) return p + i;
   return NULL;
}
```

   In the last return-statement, *NULL* is implicitly converted to type pointer-to-struct-person. We could have prescribed this conversion explicitly by means of a cast, writing

   *return (struct person *) NULL;*

but this is not necessary. The value *NULL* (=0) can be used both to assign it to any pointer variable and to compare it with any pointer value. It is guaranteed not to point to any object.

As soon as the given length *leng* is found, the statement

> *return p + i*;

is executed. It returns the address of array element *people[i]*, although the identifier *people* is unknown here. Of course, in this return statement we could have used the expression &(*p[i]*) instead of *p + i*.

5.3 DYNAMIC MEMORY-ALLOCATION

The topic of this section often occurs in connection with structures, hence its place in this chapter. However, dynamic memory-allocation does not necessarily involve structures, as our first applications will show.

Let us assume that we have declared:

> *char *p, *malloc( ), *realloc( );*
> *int n = . . . ;*

Then the assignment statement

> *p = malloc(n);*

requests a block of memory space consisting of *n* bytes. If *n* consecutive bytes are available, the request is granted, and *p* will point to the first byte. If not, *p* obtains the value *NULL*. It is a good idea to place a test of the form

> *if (p == NULL) . . .*

after that assignment statement. If *p* has been given a value different from *NULL* the allocated block of memory can be used in the same way as if we had declared

> *char p[n];*

if that were possible. (Actually this declaration is not correct, since *n* is not a constant.) Thus we can then use the *n* character variables

> *$*p, *(p + 1), . . . , *(p + n - 1)$*

or, in an equivalent notation,

> $p[0], p[1], . . . , p[n - 1]$

Note that this provides us with two new facilities. First, we can use any integer expression as an argument of *malloc* instead of only a constant-expression in an array declaration. Second, *malloc* gives us more freedom with respect to the place where we reserve memory, as the following example shows:

> *scanf("%d", &n);*
> *if (n < N) p = malloc(n); else . . .*

There is another useful facility which provides us with what we might call *flexible arrays*. Besides *malloc*, we can use the function *realloc*, which is capable of increasing or decreasing the space that has been allocated previously. For example, we can write

$$p = realloc(p, n1);$$

The first argument of *realloc* is a pointer to the block of memory of which the size is to be altered. Its second argument *n1* specifies the new size. Again, the value returned by this function will be *NULL* if memory-allocation fails. If it succeeds, the returned value is again a pointer to the first byte, and the old bytes have the same contents as before. Thus if *n1* is greater than the old-size *n* the values of

$$p[0], p[1], \ldots, p[n-1]$$

are not changed by the call of *realloc*. (This is not obvious, since the new character-sequence of length *n1* may lie somewhere else in memory, so the first *n* characters may have to be copied.)

Finally, the memory thus allocated can be released by the standard function *free*, as, for example, by

$$free(p);$$

which can be written instead of

$$realloc(p, 0);$$

So far, we have allocated memory for a sequence of characters, but it is not difficult to use *malloc* for other purposes. Suppose that at some place in the program we have computed some positive integer value *m* and we want to allocate memory for a sequence of *m* numbers of type double. Remember that *malloc* requires the amount of memory space to be expressed in bytes, so we need to know how many bytes are occupied by an object of type double. This question is properly answered by the expression

$$sizeof(double)$$

Instead, we may write

$$sizeof(xx)$$

where *xx* is an expression of type double. Syntactically, *sizeof* is a unary operator, so, if not required by precedence rules, the parentheses in the latter form may be omitted. Thus if *xx* is a variable we may write

$$sizeof\ xx$$

However, if we use a type, such as the keyword *double*, we have a special construction, in which the parentheses are required. In general, the expression

$$sizeof(\text{some type})$$

has a value equal to the number of bytes occupied by an object of the indicated type. Notice that this value may not be the same for different machines; even if we know, for example, that *sizeof(double)* yields the value 8 on our machine, it is unwise to replace *sizeof(double)* with that value, since then our program may not run properly on another machine.

We now revert to our objective of allocating memory for *m* objects of type double. If we have declared

> *double ∗pd;*
> *char ∗malloc( );*

we can write

> *pd = (double ∗)malloc(m ∗ sizeof(double));*

The cast (*double ∗*) converts pointer-to-char to pointer-to-double. Even though such a conversion may not involve any actual change in the internal representation of the pointer, if we omit the cast the compiler may complain about incompatible types in an assignment. If the request for memory is granted (which ought to be checked as before) we can use the *m* double-precision objects

> *∗pd, ∗(pd + 1), . . . , ∗(pd + m − 1),*

also accessible as

> *pd[0], pd[1], . . . , pd[m − 1]*

5.4 LINKED LISTS

In this and in the next section we shall combine dynamic memory-allocation with structures. Since structure members may have different types, we can include members which are pointers to other structures. For example, consider the linked list of Fig. 5.1. Starting at pointer variable *p*, we can reach the list element, also called a node, which contains the number 1 (in the example). Besides an information field (here an integer), each node contains a field where a pointer to the next node is located. An exception is the last node, which contains *NULL* in the pointer field.

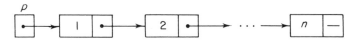

Fig. 5.1 Linked list

Let us begin with a very simple program, where we build the linked list of Fig. 5.1 for the fixed value *n* = 2:

```
/* LIST2: A linear list of only two elements */
#define NULL 0
main( )
{ struct node { int num; struct node *next; };
  typedef struct node NODE;
  NODE *p, *q;
  char *malloc( );
  int k = sizeof(NODE);
  p = (NODE *)NULL;
  q = p; p = (NODE *)malloc(k); p -> num = 2; p -> next = q;
  q = p; p = (NODE *)malloc(k); p -> num = 1; p -> next = q;
  . . .
}
```

Intentionally, we have used two almost identical lines in this program fragment. It is strongly recommended to analyse them step by step, and to sketch the resulting linear list. It will then be clear how we can generalize these two lines to a loop which produces the linear list of Fig. 5.1 for arbitrary n:

```
for (i = n; i > 0; i−−)
{ q = p; p = (NODE *)malloc(k); p−>num = i; p−>next = q;
}
```

5.5 BINARY TREES

Figure 5.2 shows a so-called *binary tree*. In general, this is composed of a pointer variable, called the *root* of the tree, and a number of nodes with some information fields and precisely two fields that can contain pointers to other nodes. Again, the pointer fields can be *NULL* instead. In Fig. 5.2 each node has only one information field, containing an integer. If a node contains pointers to other nodes, these latter nodes are said to be the *sons* of the former. If a node has sons we call it their *father*. We distinguish between a left-hand and a right-hand son. The binary tree in Fig. 5.2 has the special property that each father contains an integer which is both greater than the integer in the left-hand son and less than that in the right-hand son, if any.

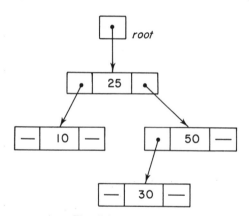

Fig. 5.2. Binary tree

As this property enables us to search the tree efficiently for a given number, the tree is sometimes called a *binary search tree*. With the aid of recursive functions operations such as building and searching such a tree involve surprisingly little program code. We shall show a program which reads a sequence of integers and builds a binary search tree for them. The input sequence is closed by the number 0, which is not stored in the tree. We shall then print the numbers stored in the tree, in ascending order. Finally, another number is read and searched for in the tree:

```
/* BINTREE: This program builds a binary search tree, and
              prints its contents in ascending order.   */
#define NULL 0
struct node { int num; struct node *left, *right; };
typedef struct node NODE;

main( )
```

```
{ int i;
  NODE *root, *ptr, *build( ), *found( );
  root = NULL;
  printf("Enter non-zero integers, followed by 0: \n");
  while (scanf("%d", &i), i) root = build(root, i);
  printf("\nIn ascending order, we have: \n");
  printtree(root);
  printf("\nEnter a number to be searched for: ");
  scanf("%d", &i);
  if (ptr = found(root, i), ptr == NULL)
     printf("Not stored. \n"); else printf("Found! \n");
}

NODE *build(p, i) NODE *p; int i;
{ char *malloc( );
  if (p == NULL)
  { p = (NODE *)malloc(sizeof(NODE));
    p -> num = i;
    p -> left = p -> right = NULL;
  } else
  if (i < p -> num) p -> left = build(p -> left, i);
                    else p -> right = build(p -> right, i);
  return p;
}

printtree(p) NODE *p;
{ if (p != NULL)
  { printtree(p -> left);
    printf("%9d\n", p -> num);
    printtree(p -> right);
  }
}

NODE *found(p, i) NODE *p; int i;
{ return
  p == NULL || i == p -> num ? p :
     found((i < p -> num ? p -> left : p -> right), i);
}
```

Here is a demonstration of this program:

Enter non-zero integers, followed by 0:
34   56   10   5   1000   23   0

In ascending order, we have:
```
        5
       10
       23
       34
       56
     1000
```

Enter a number to be searched for: 56
Found!

In real applications of binary search trees we usually search for a key, which is either an integer or, more often, a character string. Besides the key, the information that we actually want is then stored in the same node. This is why the function *found* should yield a pointer. It is through this pointer that the desired information field is then accessible for subsequent use. An example is a telephone directory, where the names are the keys, so a given name is looked up in the tree, and the telephone number stored in the same node is then accessible.

5.6 BIT FIELDS

Sometimes, in a structure, we wish to use some bits as *flags*. Although in principle all we want can be accomplished by means of the bit operators &, |, ^, ≪, ≫, ~ (discussed in Section 2.5) the language offers a facility to use individual bits more conveniently.

Suppose that in personal data the following properties are to be recorded, where, as usual, we use the codes 1 = *true* and 0 = *false*:

name	(at most 30 characters)
male	(1 or 0)
married	(1 or 0)
elderly	(1 or 0)

If, for example, we wish to declare an array of 1000 elements, each containing these four items, we can write

```
struct person
{ char name[31];
    unsigned male: 1, married: 1, elderly: 1;
} people[1000];
```

The members *male, married* and *elderly* are so-called *bit fields*. The 1 following the colon indicates that each of these fields consists of only one bit, so these structure members can only have the values 0 or 1. For example,

```
people[999]. married = 0;
```

is a valid assignment statement. Instead of 1, a greater number of bits may be chosen, but, at most, the number of bits in a single machine word (often 16 or 32). Usually bit fields occupy little space in memory. In our example the fields *male, married* and *elderly* may be bits of a single machine word. As a consequence, they have no address of their own, so we cannot use pointers to them. In our example,

```
&(person[i]. married)
```

is therefore not a valid expression. In general, a structure may contain gaps of unused memory space. So we only know that the amount of memory space occupied by a structure is at least as large as the sum of the sizes of its members. This applies to all structures, not only to those which contain bit fields. In our last example the amount of memory space for a single array element can be inquired by means of

 sizeof(struct person) or *sizeof(people[0])* etc.

5.7 UNIONS

With structures all members are physically present in memory space at the same time. For some applications this is not necessary because at each moment only one of them contains useful information. Stated differently, it is then sufficient to have *variants* rather than members, where variants occupy the same memory space. This is accomplished by so-called *unions*. Syntactically, unions are similar to structures. In the following example the variable *u* is a union, whose value is an integer or a floating-point number or a string of eight positions:

```
union intfloatstring
{ int i;
  float f;
  char str[8];
} u, *p;
```

As with structures, a tag such as *intfloatstring* is optional. The example also shows a pointer variable *p*, which can point to an object of type *union intfloatstring*. It will actually do so after the execution of

 p = &u;

As with structures, the following notations are valid:

```
u. i      u. f      u. str
p - > i   p - > f   p - > str
```

After the execution of

 u. i = 123; u. f = 3.14;

the value 123 is overwritten by 3.14 since *u. i* occupies the same memory space as *u. f,* or at least part of it. In principle, a union occupies as much memory space as its largest variant. However, if we actually need this information it is safer not to count on this but to use

 sizeof(u) or *sizeof(union intfloatstring)*

In the latter expression the tag *intfloatstring* must be preceded by the keyword *union*. It can also be used in connection with functions, as, for example, in

```
union intfloatstring *fun( )
{ . . .
}
```

where the function *fun* returns a pointer to a union of the above type. Again, note the similarity in notation of unions and structures.

5.8 EXAMPLES

Example 1

Write a program to manipulate a linked list, the nodes of which contain the triples

    n, x, y

consisting of a unique (non-negative) number *n* and the two-dimensional rectangular co-ordinates *x, y* of a point. Of course, each node (except the final one) also contains a reference to the next node. The program must be able to build and update the list, such that its elements are arranged in ascending order of point number *n*. As input we accept both triples and single-point numbers preceded by a minus sign. The latter means that the node with that number has to be removed from the list. When a triple is read, it is added to the list in the position where it belongs, unless a node with the same point number *n* is already in the list. In that case the old (*x, y*) co-ordinate pair is overwritten by the new one. Thus we can add, delete and change items in the list. A line with only the character # signals the end of the input. When this signal is read, the contents of the linked list are printed. Since the nodes are in ascending order of point number *n*, their contents will be printed in that order. Before studying program *LINKEDLIST* the reader is advised to look at the demonstration that follows it:

```
/* LINKEDLIST: An ordered linked list is built. Additions, deletions and
                  changes can be given in any order */

#define NULL 0
main( )
{ struct node { int num; float x, y; struct node *next; };
  typedef struct node NODE;
  NODE *start, *p, *q, *sentinel;
  char *malloc( );
  int k = sizeof(NODE)   , n, nabs;
  float x, y;
  start = sentinel = (NODE *)malloc(k);
  printf("Enter triples n x y to add or change, \n");
  printf("or −n to delete items in the list. \n");
  printf("Enter # to signal end of input. \n\n");
  while (scanf("%d", &n))
  { nabs = abs(n);
    sentinel −> num = nabs;
    p = start;
    while (p −> num < nabs) p = p −> next;
    if (n >= 0)
    { scanf("%f %f", &x, &y);
      if (p == sentinel)
        sentinel = p −> next = (NODE *)malloc(k);
      if (p −> num == n)
```

```
        { /* If p == sentinel then num is a new point number,
               larger than those which are already in the list,
               otherwise an existing node is changed:                    */
            p->x = x; p->y = y;
        } else        /* Insert new node just before *p:                 */
        { q = (NODE *)malloc(k);
            /* Move contents of *p to new node *q:                       */
            *q = *p;
            /* The new data are now inserted before node *q              */
            p->num = n; p->x = x; p->y = y; p->next = q;
        }
    } else
    { /* A number n < 0 is given so node *p is deleted:                  */
        if (p != sentinel)
        { q = p->next;
            *p = *q;
            if (sentinel == q) sentinel = p;
            free(q);
        }
    }
}
printf("\nResult: \n");
for (p = start; p != sentinel; p = p->next)
    printf("%6d %5.1f %5.1f\n", p->num, p->x, p->y);
}
```

Here is a demonstration of this program:

*Enter triples n x y to add or change,
or −n to delete items in the list.
Enter # to signal end of input.*

```
 2     8.5  7.3
 9     6.0  4.5
-2
 3     4.9  6.8
 8     2.2  6.6
 5     5.6  2.4
 8     1.0  1.0
 #
```

Result:

```
 3     4.9  6.8
 5     5.6  2.4
 8     1.0  1.0
 9     6.0  4.5
```

The program uses some very useful programming techniques. First, we use linear search with a *sentinel*. This means that the object to be looked for is initially placed at the end of the list, so that in the loop

> *while* $(p \rightarrow num < nabs)$ $p = p \rightarrow next$;

only a single test is needed: even if all original values *num* are less than *nabs*, the sentinel will see that the loop terminates properly. Second, when p points to a node whose *num*-value is greater than *nabs* there is a method of inserting a node containing *nabs* just before node $*p$. This is not obvious, since we apparently need a pointer to the node that precedes $*p$, and that pointer is not available. The trick is based on copying the contents of $*p$ to the new node and then placing the data to be inserted in the old node $*p$. A similar method is used for the deletion of node $*p$ without having a pointer to the node that precedes p.

Example 2

We wish to read a sequence of integers and to place them in an array. The number of integers to be read is unknown, and we will not limit that number by declaring an array of a fixed size. We shall use *realloc*, but, since *realloc* may involve copying, we shall not call this function for each new array element. Instead, we shall call this function only once for each new block of N integers, where N is 10 in this example, but probably somewhat larger in practical situations. To demonstrate this method we shall print the numbers after the character # (as an end signal) has been read:

```
/* DYNAMIC: A dynamic array */
#define N 10
#define NULL 0
main( )
{ char *malloc( ), *realloc( );
  int i, n = 0, x, *a, allocated, blocksize, intsize, inuse;

  /* allocated = number of allocated bytes          */
  /* blocksize = number of bytes in one block        */
  /* intsize   = number of bytes in one integer       */
  /* inuse     = number of bytes containing integers */

  intsize = sizeof(int); blocksize = N * intsize; inuse = 0;
  a = (int *)malloc(blocksize); allocated = blocksize;
  printf("Enter a sequence of integers, followed by #: \");
  while (scanf("%d", &x))
  { inuse += intsize;
    if (inuse > allocated)
    { allocated += blocksize;
      a = (int *)realloc(a, allocated);
      if (a == NULL) { printf("Lack of memory\n"); exit(1); }
    }
    a[n++] = x; /* n integers have been read */
  }
```

```
printf("\nallocated: %d bytes\n", allocated);
printf("blocksize: %d bytes\n", blocksize);
printf("intsize   : %d bytes\n", intsize);
printf("inuse     : %d bytes\n", inuse);
printf("n         : %d integers\n\n", n);
printf("Here are the numbers: \n");
for (i = 0; i < n; i++)
    printf("%5d%c", a[i], i % 10 == 9 ? '\n' : ' ');
printf("\n");
}
```

In the following demonstration several interesting quantities have been printed as well. It shows that the program was run on a system where an integer occupies four bytes:

Enter a sequence of integers, followed by #:

1	2	3	4	5	6	7	8	9	10
11	12	13	14	15	16	17	18	19	20
21	22	23	24	25	26	27	28		
#									

Allocated: 120 *bytes*
blocksize: 40 *bytes*
intsize   : 4 *bytes*
inuse   : 112 *bytes*
n   : 28 *integers*

Here are the numbers:

	1	2	3	4	5	6	7	8	9	10
	11	12	13	14	15	16	17	18	19	20
	21	22	23	24	25	26	27	28		

5.9 EXERCISES

5.1   A program is to read some buffer size n, followed by a (potentially infinite) sequence of pairs c, i, where c is a command and i is an integer. There are two possible commands:

    A *i*: Add integer i to the buffer and remove the least recently read integer, if necessary for having at most n integers in the buffer.

    P *k*: Print the kth last number that was read ($k \leq n$).

Use a linked list to store the n most recently read integers.

5.2   The given values x_{min}, x_{max}, y_{min}, y_{max} determine a rectangle with inner points (x, y) satisfying

$$x_{min} < x < x_{max}$$
$$y_{min} < y < y_{max}$$

Also, a constant N is given, to divide the rectangle into $N \times N$ elementary rectangles, all of the same size. The co-ordinates (x, y) of a great many points, all lying inside the rectangle, are to be read and then stored in $N \times N$ linked lists each of which starts in an element of two-dimensional array P of pointers. More specifically, point (x, y) is stored in the linked list starting in $P[i][j]$, where i and j are the truncated values of $N \cdot (x - x_{min})/(x_{max} - x_{min})$ and $N \cdot (y - y_{min})/(y_{max} - y_{min})$, respectively. Each node can simply be added at the beginning of the linked list where it belongs, so the order of the nodes in a list is irrelevant. To demonstrate the program, print the contents of all linked lists.

5.3   Write a program which reads the number n, followed by n integers, in ascending order. For example:

　　6
　　10   12   35   40   50   55

These n integers are to be stored in a perfectly balanced binary search tree. A binary tree is said to be *perfectly balanced* if, for each node, the number of nodes in its left-hand and its right-hand subtree differ by at most one. Figure 5.3 shows a perfectly balanced binary search tree for the six integers in the example.

　　Use a recursive function with one integer argument, which indicates how many integers are to be read and stored. The function is to return the root of the tree it has built. If its argument is positive, the function performs two recursive calls, namely one for each of its subtrees. Between these two calls it reads one number itself and stores this in a newly created node. Demonstrate the program with the aid of another recursive function, which prints the numbers stored in the tree in such a way that the tree structure will be reflected by indentation. Figure 5.4 is an example of such tree representation, which is in fact the tree of Fig. 5.3 turned through 90 degrees in the positive sense.

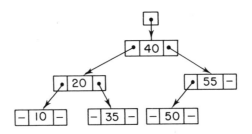

Fig. 5.3. A perfectly balanced binary tree

```
                    55
                        50
            40
                        35
                20
                    10
```

Fig. 5.4. Tree-representation by indentation

CHAPTER 6

More on input and output

6.1 INTRODUCTION

For input and output we do not use any special statements, so from a syntactic point of view nothing new will be presented in this chapter. All we need is a library of standard I/O functions. In addition to this library, it is convenient to use an include file with some declarations and definitions which we would otherwise have to write ourselves. This file is the well-known header file *stdio. h,* included by the program line

> *#include ⟨stdio. h⟩*

In Sections 2.12 and 3.6 our discussion of some I/O functions and macros was far from complete. In this chapter we shall study most of the I/O facilities belonging to what is known as *standard input and output.* They are available in almost all C implementations, so by using only these facilities our programs will be more portable than by using low-level routines associated with the operating system that is used. On the other hand, in special cases there may be very good reasons to use those system-dependent routines as well, and even the 'standard' facilities dealt with in this chapter might be available on our machine in a slightly different form, so we should consult the reference manual of our C implementation.

6.2 FORMAT STRINGS FOR *PRINTF*

We often say that a value is *printed* in cases where the latter term should not be taken literally but may, for example, denote output on the screen of a terminal. The functions *printf, sprintf* and *fprintf,* discussed in this chapter, produce results which may eventually be printed on paper, but in most cases a hard copy is not needed and we can use those functions even if no printer is available at all! A call of the function *printf* has the form

> *printf (format-string, arg1, arg2, . . .)*

where zero or more arguments *argi* may follow the first argument *format-string.* The format string need not be a string constant, as the following examples show:

> *char str[. . .]; int i = . . . ;*
> *. . .*
> *printf (str, . . .)*
> *printf (str + i, . . .)*
> *printf (i < 0 ? "Negative" : (i > 0 ? "Positive" : "Zero"));*

In the (value of the) format string two kind of objects may occur:

(1) Characters to be printed literally;
(2) Conversion specifications.

The format string must contain as many conversion specifications as there are subsequent arguments *arg*1, *arg*2, ... The first conversion specification is matched with *arg*1, the second with *arg*2, and so on. Each conversion specification begins with a per cent sign (%) and ends with a conversion character. Some information may occur between the per cent sign and the conversion character, as discussed below, but first we list the conversion characters themselves:

d The argument is converted to decimal format.

o The argument is converted to unsigned octal format, without a leading zero.

x The argument is converted to unsigned hexadecimal format, without leading $0x$. A small letter x causes small letters $a, \ldots, f$ to appear as hexadecimal digits. Use capital X if capital letters $A, \ldots, F$ are desired.

u The argument is converted to unsigned decimal format.

c The argument is printed as a single character.

s The argument is a pointer to a character. From the first character, all characters are printed until a null character is encountered or as many characters have been printed as the precision (inserted between % and s) indicates.

f The argument is floating (float or double) and it is converted to decimal format of the form $[-]mmm.nnn$, where both the field width and the precision are specified between % and f. If this information is absent (that is, if the format specification is %f) the default precision value is 6.

e The argument is floating and it is converted to the decimal format $[-]m.nnnnnne\{\pm\}xx$, where xx denotes the exponent of a power of ten. The precision, that is, the number of digits n, may be specified between % and e. The default precision is 6. Use E instead of e if a capital E in the result, is preferred.

g The shorter of the results obtained by f and e is chosen.

Between the per cent sign and the conversion character the following may occur:

(1) A minus sign $(-)$, which means that the converted argument is to appear left justified in the field that is available, so padding occurs on the right.
(2) One or more decimal digits specifying the minimum width to be used. If the result is wider than this minimum it is written anyway. If it is smaller it is padded, usually with blanks on the left. If a minus sign is specified, padding occurs on the right. Instead of blanks, zeros are used as padding characters if the given minimum width is preceded by a zero. If no field width is specified just as many positions are used as are needed.
(3) A period (.) to separate the minimum width from the specified precision.
(4) One or more decimal digits, specifying the precision. It is the number of fractional digits with the f and e conversion characters and the number of characters with the s conversion character.
(5) The small letter l, to be used if the argument is long.

As an example with a minus sign, a width (14) and a precision (11), consider the program

```
main( )
{ printf ("?%14. 11s!\n", "Instructive example");
  printf ("?%−14. 11s!\n", "Instructive example");
}
```

which produce the following output:

?   *Instructive*!
?*Instructive*   !

The three characters ?, ! and \n in the format strings occur outside format specifications, and are therefore printed literally. We can write %% if a per cent sign is to be printed.

When using *printf* we have to take care that the types of the arguments to be printed correspond to the conversion character used for it: %d, %o, %x, %u, %c may only match integral arguments and %f, %e, %g may only match floating arguments. Recall that the term integral includes type char. If %d is used for a char value, the decimal representation of the internal value of that character will be printed. To print the character itself, we use %c.

For the sake of completeness, it should be mentioned that *printf* returns a value equal to the number of characters transmitted or a negative value if an output error was encountered.

6.3 FORMAT STRINGS FOR *SCANF*

The function *scanf* reads data from the keyboard. Two other functions, *sscanf* and *fscanf*, are similar to *scanf* with respect to format-conversion. A call of the function *scanf* has the form

scanf (*format-string, arg1, arg1, . . .*)

The arguments *arg1, arg2, . . .* are pointers telling us where the information that is read is to be stored. Probably the most common error in C is forgetting this pointer aspect and writing something like

scanf ("%d", n)

instead of

scanf ("%d", &n)

The above calls of *scanf* are deliberately not followed by a semicolon, for that would suggest that we use them as statements, ignoring the returned value. However, in many cases that value is very useful. It is the number of input items read into the objects pointed to by *arg1, arg2, . . .* We can use it to test whether the read attempt has succeeded. In particular, the value 0 is returned if the next input character does not match the first format specification. If nothing can be read because of end-of-file, the returned value will be *EOF*, usually defined in *stdio. h* as −1.

As with *printf*, each conversion specification begins with a per cent sign, possibly followed by some optional characters, and it ends with a conversion character. Here is a list of conversion characters for *scanf*:

> *d* A decimal representation of an integer is expected. The type of the corresponding argument must be pointer-to-int. Use *hd* or *ld* if the argument is a pointer to short or to long, respectively (see below).
>
> *o* An octal representation of an integer is expected. There need not be a leading zero.
>
> *x* A hexadecimal representation of an integer is expected, with or without leading 0*x*.
>
> *c* A single character is expected.
>
> *s* A sequence of characters (a string) is expected. At the beginning, any white-space characters are skipped. If no field width is inserted between % and *s* (see below) the string will be read until a white-space character is encountered.
>
> *f* A floating-point number is expected, but an integer such as, for example, −123 is accepted as well. The type of the corresponding argument must be pointer-to-float. If it is pointer-to-double, use *lf* (see below).

A field width may be inserted between the per cent sign and the conversion character; if present, as many characters are read as the field width indicates. Since we usually want so-called *free-format* input, a field width is specified less frequently for input than for output.

The conversion characters *d, o, x* must be preceded by *h* if the corresponding argument has type pointer-to-short, and by *l* in case of pointer-to-long. Furthermore, the letter *l* must be used immediately before *f* if the corresponding argument has type pointer-to-double. An inserted asterisk, as, for example, in % * *d*, indicates that although reading is to take place, no assignment is made and there is no corresponding pointer argument: in other words, a value in the input stream has to be skipped.

Outside conversion specifications the format string of *scanf* may contain other characters. White-space characters (spaces, tabs and newline characters) match an optional sequence of white-space characters in the input stream. An ordinary character (not %) must match the next non-white character in the input stream. If we read only numbers, we normally have only conversion specifications in the format string, possibly separated by a space for reasons of program-readability. For example, if we have declared

> *short s; int i; long l; float x; double xx;*

the call

> *scanf("%hd %d %ld %f %lf", &s, &i, &l, &x, &xx)*

is equivalent to

> *scanf("%hd%d%ld%f%lf", &s, &i, &l, &x, &xx)*

In the input stream, the numbers are separated by white-space characters.

Therefore, for example, the input data

    12   12345   123456789
    3.4   −1000

are accepted by both calls of *scanf* (provided that 123456789 fits into the long int variable *l*). In this example note the distinction between *%hd* for short and *%d* for int, whereas with *printf* the same conversion specification *%d* is used for both purposes. The reason for this is that, with *printf*, short is automatically converted to int, but with *scanf* the format specification *%hd* or *%d* tells the function whether the corresponding argument is the address of either a short or an int object. Such information is needed to place the values that are read in the proper memory locations. A similar distinction can be observed between *%f* for float and *%lf* for double.

We shall also demonstrate the use of field widths. If we use

> *char str*[20]; *int i, j, n*;
> *n = scanf ("%3s %2d %d", str, &i, &j);*

the input line

    123456789*A*

will give the same values to the variables *str, i, j, n* as the following statements would:

> *strcpy (str, "123"); i = 45; j = 6789; n = 3;*

After the above call of *scanf*, the letter *A* is the next character to be read.

6.4 IN-MEMORY FORMAT-CONVERSION

In this chapter we discuss two functions which, though derived from *printf* and *scanf*, do not actually perform any input or output. When printing with *printf*, the representation of each number is converted from its binary notation, used internally, to a sequence of ASCII characters consisting of digits and special characters, including leading blanks. Sometimes we want only this conversion, not the actual output. Instead of on the screen of our terminal, the resulting character sequence is to appear in a string variable. The name of the function for this is derived from the name *printf* by writing the letter *s* (the first letter of *string*) in front of it. For example, after

> *int i = 123; char str*[8];

the statement

> *sprintf (str, "%4d", 2 ∗ i);*

will place the three digits 2, 4, 6, preceded by a blank and followed by a null character in the string variable *str* in the same way as we could have achieved by

> *strcpy (str, " 246");*

Thus, except for the null character at the end, the characters sent to *str* are the same as those which would be sent to the standard output medium by

> *printf* (*"%4d"*, 2 ∗ *i*);

When using *sprintf* (or *strcpy*) there must be enough space in the target string variable *str,* otherwise the consequences will be undefined. Another point to remember is that *str* need not actually be the name of a character array: it can also be a pointer to some character in the middle of such an array. All possibilities of *printf* with respect to formatting are also available with *sprintf*. Since both source and destination are in memory, we say that *sprintf* is a function for *in-memory format-conversion.*

The same term is used for the opposite conversion, for which the function *sscanf* is available. It is related to *scanf* in the same way as *sprintf* is related to *printf*. For example, after

> *static char str*[100] = *"1.23   45   A"*;
> *float x*;
> *int i, count*;
> *char ch*;

the statement

> *count* = *sscanf* (*str,* *"%f %d %c"*, &*x*, &*i*, &*ch*);

will have the same effect as

> *x* = 1.23; *i* = 45; *ch* = '*A*'; *count* = 3;

Note that in this example we did not ignore the value returned by *sscanf*. As with *scanf*, it is the number of successfully matched and transmitted items. The functions *printf* and *sprintf* return similar values, which are usually ignored.

6.5   FILES

So far, I/O facilities were restricted to the keyboard and the screen of our terminal, which are technically referred to as standard input (*stdin*) and standard output (*stdout*). In practical programs we often want to read from and write to a file on a disk. Such files have names known to the operating system so that we can select any file we want. In contrast to an array, the information in a file still exists after our program has terminated. For example, program *A* can write a file today and program *B* can read it tomorrow. A file does not have a predefined length; we can simply start writing in a file at its beginning, and, except for the limitations imposed by the entire disk, we can go on as long as we like. After the completion of all write operations the file length is equal to the number of bytes that have been written. The action of connecting our program to a file is called *opening* that file. Similarly, when we *close* a file our program is disconnected from it. Some very technical information about the file we are using is available in a piece of memory, which we shall call a *file-control-block*. In C terminology a file-control-block is a structure whose type is somewhat confusingly called *FILE* (in four capital letters). The header file *stdio. h,* included in our program by

> #*include ⟨stdio. h⟩*

contains a type definition of the form

> *typedef struct* { . . . } *FILE;*

(see Section 5.1 for the way we use *typedef*). Thus after the above include line we could use the identifier *FILE* to declare variables of that type. However, we actually do not declare a file-control-block itself but only a pointer to it by means of, for example,

> *FILE* **fp;*

where we call *fp* a *file pointer.* Remember that initially the value of variable *fp* is undefined and that at this stage a file-control-block does not yet exist. For any file we wish to use we create a file-control-block by opening that file. For this purpose the standard function *fopen* is available, which is called as follows:

> *fp* = *fopen(name, code);*

The first argument, *name,* is a string containing the file name, as it is known externally. The second argument is a code, for which we have the following possibilities:

"r"   Read. Only to be used for existing files.

"w"   Write. If the file already exists, its old contents are lost, otherwise the file is created.

"a"   Append. If the file does not yet exist it is created.

"r+"   Update an existing file (read and write).

"w+"   As *"w",* but reading is possible as well.

"a+"   As *"a",* but reading is possible as well.

(Besides these, more codes may be available on the reader's system; he should consult the reference manual for his C implementation.) If it is possible to open the file, *fopen* returns a pointer to the file-control-block, which in turn contains a reference to the file itself. The value returned by *fopen* is normally assigned to a file pointer, say *fp,* which is subsequently used whenever we want to communicate with the file. We shall refer to this file as the *stream fp,* as short-hand for 'the file with the file-control-block pointed to by *fp*'. An attempt to open a file may fail, which makes it desirable to check the result of such an attempt. Fortunately, if a file cannot be opened, for example if *"r"* is specified and the file does not exist, the value returned by *fopen* is *NULL.* It is therefore easy to include such a check in our program, writing, for example:

> *fp* = *fopen("EXAMPLE. DAT", "r");*
> *if (fp* == *NULL)*
> { *printf("File EXAMPLE. DAT cannot be opened\n");*
>   *exit(1);*
> }

Actual reading and writing can now be carried out with several functions, including *fscanf* and *fprintf*. Like *sscanf* and *sprintf*, they have been derived from the well-known functions *scanf* and *printf*. They expect a file pointer as their first argument:

> *fscanf(fp1, format string, data-items)*
> *fprintf(fp2, format string, data-items)*

These functions return values similar to those returned by *scanf* and *printf*. Function *fscanf* returns either the number of data items read or the negative value *EOF*, and *fprintf* returns the number of characters written.

It is now time to discuss a complete program that deals with files. Let us assume, for example, that we are given file *NUM. DAT* containing integers in readable form, that is, in the usual representation consisting of decimal digits, blanks and newline characters. The following program reads these numbers from that file and writes their absolute values to the file *ABS. DAT*. Note the way in which the end of the input file is detected:

```
/* ABSVALUE: Reads integers from file NUM. DAT, and writes
                their absolute values to file ABS. DAT          */

#include <stdio. h>
main( )
{ FILE *in, *out;
  int i;
  in = fopen("NUM. DAT", "r");
  if (in == NULL)
     { printf("can't open file NUM. DAT\n"); exit(1); }
  out = fopen("ABS. DAT", "w");
  if (out == NULL)
     { printf("can't open file ABS. DAT\n"); exit(1); }
  while (fscanf(in, "%d", &i) > 0)
     fprintf(out, "%5d\n", abs(i));
  fclose(in); fclose(out);
}
```

The last two statements of this program are superfluous if on program-termination all open files are automatically closed, which is usually the case. Still, in more complex situations the function *fclose* will be useful if we wish to close a file long before a program terminates, thus allowing other programs (or the same one!) to open it again. After the file is opened we start at its beginning, so *fclose* followed by *fopen* can be regarded as 'rewind'. Note that the above while loop terminates when *fscanf* returns a non-positive value, that is, when no number can be read. If the file contains only valid representations of integers, and the hardware works properly, program *ABSVALUE* performs its task quite satisfactorily. In other situations we can use the two functions *feof* and *ferror* to obtain information about what happened. Both have one argument, a file pointer:

> *feof(fp)*   is non-zero if the end of stream *fp* has been reached, and zero otherwise.

ferror(*fp*) is non-zero if an error has occurred while reading from or writing to
stream *fp*.

For example, in program *ABSVALUE* we can insert the following if-statement:

```
if (! feof(in))
{ printf("Reading failed in the middle of the file\n");
   exit(1);
}
```

just before the line where function *fclose* is used. This would cause a message to be
displayed if file *NUM. DAT* should contain wrong characters such as letters. The
original program, on the other hand, simply stops in that case in the same way as if
the end of the file had been reached.

Besides the functions *fscanf* and *fprintf*, similar to *scanf* and *printf*, we can use the
macros *getc* and *putc*, similar to *getchar* and *putchar*:

getc(*fp*)   has type int and returns the next character that is read from stream *fp*
             if a character can be read, and *EOF* otherwise (see below).
putc(*ch, fp*) writes character *ch* (of type int, see below) to stream *fp*.

Let us assume that a character is coded in 8 bits and an integer in 32 bits. Then
the int value yielded by *getc* will contain the character that has been read into its
least significant 8 bits. Some negative int value (usually −1), with an internal
representation distinct from all those coded characters, is called *EOF*. Its name
means End-Of-File and it is defined in the header file *stdio. h* as

```
#define EOF (−1)
```

Thus the characters are embedded in the set of the integers which gives the
possibility of including the pseudo-character *EOF*. This is why the value of *getc* is of
type int rather than char. For reasons of symmetry, the first argument of *putc* also
has type int. However, this does not prevent us from writing, for example,

```
putc('A', fp);
```

This is even perfectly correct, because a character constant such as *'A'* actually has
type int. Since C is not difficult with respect to conversion from int to char, and vice
versa, we did not mention this in Section 2.2 to avoid any confusion.

We shall demonstrate the use of *getc* and *putc* by means of a very general program
designed to copy one file to another. The names of the input and the output file, in
that order, are specified as program arguments. Note that *ch* has type int, not char:

```
/* COPY: Copies the first given file to the second */
#include ⟨stdio. h⟩
main(argc, argv) int argc; char **argv;
{ int ch;
   FILE *in, *out;
   if (argc != 3)
   { printf("Input and output file are to be specified\n");
      exit(1);
   }
```

```
in = fopen(argv[1], "r");
out = fopen(argv[2], "w");
if (in == NULL || out == NULL)
{ printf("Can't open an input and an output file\n");
   exit(1);
}
while (ch = getc(in), ch != EOF) putc(ch, out);
fclose(in); fclose(out);
}
```

Almost all the work is done by the while-statement in the third line from the bottom. In the include file *stdio. h*, the three file pointers *stdin*, *stdout* and *stderr* are defined. Their names stand for standard input, standard output and standard error devices. Normally *stdin* is associated with the keyboard, and both *stdout* and *stderr* with the screen of our terminal. They can, however, be redirected to any files, on most operating systems. We shall not discuss this any further, but, if the reader is interested, he is advised to consult the reference manual for his system.

For *stdin* and *stdout,* we have the following equivalences:

fscanf(stdin, . . .)	is equivalent to	*scanf(. . .)*
fprintf(stdout, . . .)	is equivalent to	*printf(. . .)*
getc(stdin)	is equivalent to	*getchar( )*
putc(ch, stdout)	is equivalent to	*putchar(ch)*

The opposite of *getc* is *ungetc*:

ungetc(ch, fp) pushes the character specified by *ch* back into the input stream *fp*.

6.6 LINE INPUT AND OUTPUT

To read and write an entire line we use the functions *fgets*, *fputs*, *gets*, *puts*. Their returned values and their arguments will now be discussed using the same notation as in Section 4.9. If we wish to use the functions we have to include the file *stdio. h*.

*char *fgets(str, n, fp) char *str; int n; FILE *fp;*

At most, $n - 1$ characters are read from the stream *fp* into the array *str*. If a newline character is read it is placed in the string and no additional characters are read. A null character is placed immediately after the last character read into the array. If end-of-file is encountered and no characters have been read into the array, the pointer value *NULL* is returned, otherwise the pointer value *str* is returned.

*int fputs(str, fp) char *str; FILE *fp;*

String *str* is written to stream *fp*. If at the end of the string a newline character is to be written, it has to be present in the string *str*. The terminating null character is not copied to the output stream. The function returns non-zero if an error occurs; otherwise it returns zero.

*char *gets(str) char *str;*

From the stream *stdin* characters are read into the array *str* until a newline character is read. The newline character is not placed into the array. A null character is written immediately after the last character read into the array.

int puts(*str*) *char* ∗*str*;

String *str* is written to stream *stdout*, followed by a newline character. The function returns non-zero if an error occurs; otherwise it returns zero.

As an example here is a program which reads all lines of the file *ABC* and copies only those lines which are longer than 20 positions. The copied lines appear both in file *ABCLONG* and on stream *stdout* (that is, on the screen):

```
/* COPYLONG: This program copies all lines of more than 20 characters (not
                   including the newline character, which also is copied).     */
#include ⟨stdio. h⟩

main( )
{ FILE *in, *out;
  char str[200], *p;
  int length;
  in = fopen("ABC", "r"); out = fopen("ABCLONG", "w");
  if (in == NULL || out == NULL) exit(1);
  while (p = fgets(str, 200, in), p != NULL)
  { if (length = strlen(str) − 1, length > 20)
      { fputs(str, out);
        str[length] = '\0';
        puts(str);
      }
  }
  fclose(in); fclose(out);
}
```

For example, a line with only the two letters *X* and *Y* leads to *strlen*("*XY\n*"), which has the value 3. So we have to decrease the value of *strlen*(*str*) by one to find *length*, the number of characters that precede the newline character. If *length* is greater than 20, the contents of *str*, up to and including the newline characters, are written by means of *fputs*. Since these characters count from zero, the newline character is located in position *length*. Before we send *str* to *stdout* by means of *puts*, that newline character has to be overwritten by a null character, for *puts* itself adds a newline character, and we must avoid writing two of them. We have used *puts* here to illustrate this very aspect, for a simpler solution would have been to use *fputs* for *stdout* as well. Instead of

str[*length*] = '\0';
puts(*str*);

we could then simply have written:

fputs(*str*, *stdout*);

In this example we have assumed that each line, including a newline character and a null character, will not be longer than 200 positions.

6.7 UNFORMATTED I/O AND DIRECT-ACCESS

Besides *fscanf* and *fprintf* for formatted I/O we have the functions *fread* and *fwrite* for unformatted input and output. If numbers are to be written to a file it is not always necessary to represent them by a sequence of ASCII characters such as decimal digits. If the data are only stored with the purpose of reading them afterwards by another (or the same) program it is more efficient to write them in the same format as coded internally. For example, the integer 19 is often represented internally as a sequence of the following 32 bits:

> 0000   0000   0000   0000   0000   0000   0001   0011

We can write a sequence like this to a file using the function *fwrite* as follows:

> *int i* = 19;
> *FILE* *fp*;
> *fp* = *fopen*(...);
> . . .
> *fwrite*(&*i*, *sizeof*(*int*), 1, *fp*);

In general, we have:

> *fread*(*bufptr*, *size*, *n*, *fp*)
> *fwrite*(*bufptr*, *size*, *n*, *fp*)

where the arguments have the following meaning:

> *bufptr*   A pointer to a buffer (the address of an object in memory).
> *size*   The size (in bytes) of one element in the buffer.
> *n*   The number of elements in the buffer.
> *fp*   A file pointer.

Both functions return an int value, which is the number of items actually read or written, so normally it will be equal to *n*, the third argument. We can use the value of *fread* to test whether a read attempt has failed, in which case that value is less than *n*. If nothing at all can be read, possibly due to end-of-file, the returned value is 0, not *EOF*. To distinguish end-of-file from a read error, we can use at least one of the functions *feof* and *ferror*.

So far, all I/O was sequential: we have read from and written to a file in one direction, from its beginning to its end. However, in many applications we may wish to perform I/O operations on the file items in any order we like, in the same way as we can access the elements of an array. The technical term for this is *direct access* (or random access), which is the opposite of sequential access. Using direct access we often wish to update a file, that is, to read an item, modify it and write it back. The latter is possible if we write "*r+*" rather than "*r*" as the second argument of *fopen*, as mentioned in the previous section. (Our implementation may require still other strings for this purpose, as we shall see at the end of this section.) To locate a position in a file, we use a call of the function *fseek*:

> *fseek*(*fp*, *offset*, *code*)

with the following arguments

fp   File pointer.

offset The position, expressed in bytes, relative to a point specified by the third argument *code*; *offset* has type long int.

code 0: *offset* is relative to the beginning of the file (*offset* = 0 denotes the first position of the file).

   1: *offset* is relative to the current position (for example, *offset* = -1 moves back one byte).

   2: *offset* is relative to the end of the file (and must therefore be negative).

The function *fseek* returns zero if the call was successful; otherwise it returns non-zero.

We can also inquire what the current position is by

   ftell(fp)

The *long* int value returned by *ftell* is the offset to be used later as the second argument of *fseek* (with *code* = 0) if we wish to return to the same position in the stream *fp*.

Since file-access methods have much to do with the operating system that is used it is wise to consult the reference manual for our C compiler, especially if the system distinguishes between binary files and text files (also called ASCII files). The programs in this book were executed on a PRIME computer, running under the PRIMOS operating system, where this distinction is made. The only point which reflects this distinction is the second argument of *fopen,* discussed in the previous section. In contrast to other C implementations, the PRIME C compiler here requires the letters *i* and *o* to be used instead of *r* and *w,* respectively, for I/O on binary files (*r* and *w* being reserved for ASCII files). The reason is that on ASCII files a compression technique is used for long sequences of space characters. For direct-access, however, the position where we want to read or write has to be calculated, and thus space-compression must not take place.

We have discussed these details for two reasons. First, it is instructive to have an example of how various C implementations might diverge, and second, it is always good practice to list programs exactly in the same form as they actually have been executed. This is why in the next section the letters *i* and *o* appear in the second argument of *fopen*.

6.8 EXAMPLES

When dealing with a great many objects of the same structure type we often call these objects *records*. In accordance with what frequently occurs in practice, we shall now use files of records. Though usually rather long in real applications, our records will be very simple. As in the beginning of Chapter 5, they consist of three members, called *name, year* and *length*. Since several programs will use the same structure type it is very convenient to define this type in a header file, and to include this file, writing

   #include "PERSFILE. H"

each time we need that structure type. Here are the contents of the file *PERSFILE. H*:

```
#define NAME_LENGTH 30
typedef struct
        { char name[NAME_LENGTH + 1];
          int year, length;
        } PERSON;
```

Actually, this file defines five identifiers, namely the constant *NAME_LENGTH*, the type *PERSON*, and the three member names *name, year, length*. We shall include this header file in Examples 1–4. Very briefly, these show how a file of records can be generated, printed, sorted and searched, respectively. Example 4 demonstrates direct access combined with updating.

Example 1

Write a program which generates a given number of records of type *PERSON*. Use a random number generator for the actual name lengths, the names themselves, the years (of birth) and the lengths. Of course, we cannot expect well-known surnames to be generated but instead we are satisfied with any sequence of capital letters. The years to be generated will range from 1920 to 1969, lengths from 130 to 199 (cm). The file generated is not completely useless, since it will provide the input data for an interesting sort program, to be discussed in Example 3. We could, of course, have used well-known surnames, but these would have to be entered manually, whereas the following program only asks how many records of persons we want, so we can very easily obtain a quite extensive file:

```
/* GENFIL: Generation of a test file consisting of records with one string and
                two int members                                                */
#include <stdio. h>
#include "PERSFILE. H"
main( )
{ int n, i, j, len;
  PERSON a;
  FILE *fp;
  printf("How many persons? "); scanf("%d", &n);
  srand(12345);
  fp = fopen("PEOPLE", "o");
  for (i = 0; i < n; i++)
  { len = 1 + rand( ) % NAME_LENGTH;
    for (j = 0; j < = NAME_LENGTH; j++)
      a. name[j] = (j < len ? 'A' + rand( ) % 26 : '\0');
    a. year = 1920 + rand( ) % 50;
    a. length = 130 + rand( ) % 70;
    fwrite(&a, sizeof(a), 1, fp);
    printf("%-30s %4d %3d\n", a. name, a. year, a. length);
  }
  fclose(fp);
}
```

This program creates the file *PEOPLE,* and writes as many records to it as we specify. To this end, the function *fwrite* is used. We have also included a line which sends the same data to *stdout,* so that we can see immediately what data are written to the file. As usual, *printf* is used for this purpose; it gives formatted output, so numbers appear as readable characters. In contrast to this, *fwrite* gives unformatted output, which implies that the file *PEOPLE* cannot be printed in the usual way, but can only be made readable by a special program (see Example 2). Note how the remainder operator % is used to obtain integers in a desired range. For example, the value of

rand( ) % 50

is one of the integers $0, 1, \ldots, 49$.

Example 2

Write a program which prints the contents of files such as those generated in Example 1. The file name has to be supplied as a program argument, so that we can apply the program not only to the file *PEOPLE* but also to similar files. Here is the program:

```
/* PRINTPERSONS: This program reads a file of records of type PERSON
                  and prints the contents                         */
#include 〈stdio. h〉
#include "PERSFILE. H"

main(argc, argv) int argc; char **argv;
{ FILE *fp;
  PERSON a;
    if (argc != 2)
        { printf("Program arguments!\n"); exit(1); }
    fp = fopen(argv[1], "i"); /* Implementation dependent */
    if (fp == NULL { printf("File not open\n"); exit(1); }
    while (fread(&a, sizeof(a), 1, fp))
        printf("%-30s %4d %4d\n", a. name, a. year, a. length);
    fclose(fp);
}
```

Example 3

Write a program which sorts the file *PEOPLE* such that the names will be in alphabetic order. We shall use the method known as *natural-merge sort.* An extensive discussion of this method is beyond the scope of this book, so we shall deal with it in a practical way and refrain from comparing its performance with other external sorting methods. Let us, for convenience, use numbers instead of strings in this explanation. Suppose we are given the following sequence *f*:

28   50   33   15   20   100   35   40   17

Although these numbers were chosen at random, there are subsequences in increasing order, as indicated; such a subsequence is called a *run*. (If the whole sequence is in decreasing order, there are only runs of length 1.) We now distribute the numbers, forming two new sequences g and h, such that alternately complete runs are copied, first to sequence g, second to sequence h, third to sequence g again, and so on. Thus we obtain:

g: 28   50   15   20   100   17

h: 33   35   40

(Note that the two runs {33} and {35, 40} of sequence f spontaneously form only one run in sequence h. This is not a problem at all, since g and h need not contain the same number of runs.) After this distribution phase the sequences g and h are merged into one, which we call f again. Repeatedly, a run of g and a run of h are merged into one run, written to f. So after this merge phase we have the same numbers in f as before, but in fewer and longer runs. We now repeat the whole process, distributing and merging again, and so on, until there is only one run in f.

Although this principle is rather simple it is not so easy to write a program for it. We have to determine the end of a run, which is either near the beginning of a new run or at the end of the file. If a new run follows, its first element must be read to decide this, but we cannot immediately use it because the current runs have to be dealt with first. For these reasons the complexity of the program should not surprise us. However, it is a good exercise to study the program carefully, or, even better, to write one! The computing time for this method is roughly proportional to $n \log n$, where n is the number of records. This means that the method can be used in practice for quite extensive files. Here is the program:

```
/* NATMSORT: Natural Merge Sort */
#include ⟨stdio. h⟩
#include "PERSFILE. H"
FILE *f, *g, *h;
int number_of_runs, size = sizeof(PERSON);

main( )
{ do
    { distribute( ); /* f is read, g and h are written */
      merge( );
    } while (number_of_runs > 1);
}

distribute( )
{ PERSON a;
  f = fopen("PEOPLE", "i");
  g = fopen("AUX1", "o");
  h = fopen("AUX2", "o");
  fread(&a, size, 1, f);
  while (! feof(f))
  { copy_a_run(f, g, &a); if (feof(f)) break;
    copy_a_run(f, h, &a);
  }
```

```
        fclose(f); fclose(g); fclose(h);
    }

    copy_a_run(in, out, pnext) FILE *in, *out; PERSON *pnext;
    { PERSON old;
        do
        { fwrite(pnext, size, 1, out);
          old = *pnext;
          fread(pnext, size, 1, in);
        } while (!(feof(in) || strcmp(pnext -> name, old. name) < 0));
        number_of_runs ++;
    }

    merge( )
    { PERSON ag, ah, old;
        number_of_runs = 0;
        f = fopen("PEOPLE", "o");
        g = fopen("AUX1", "i"); h = fopen("AUX2", "i");
        fread(&ag, size, 1, g); fread(&ah, size, 1, h);
        while (!feof(g) && !feof(h))
        { if (strcmp(ag. name, ah. name) < 0)
            { fwrite(&ag, size, 1, f);
              old = ag;
              fread(&ag, size, 1, g);
              if (feof(g) || strcmp(ag. name, old. name) < 0)
                copy_a_run(h, f, &ah);
            } else
            { fwrite(&ah, size, 1, f);
              old = ah;
              fread(&ah, size, 1, h);
              if (feof(h) || strcmp(ah. name, old. name) < 0)
                copy_a_run(g, f, &ag);
            }
        }
        while (!feof(g)) copy_a_run(g, f, &ag);
        while (!feof(h)) copy_a_run(h, f, &ah);
        fclose (f); fclose(g); fclose(h);
    }
```

The function *copy_a_run* does what its name says, with two exceptions. First, when it is called, the first element of the run to be copied has already been read. Second, after copying a run, the first element of the next run has already been read, if there is one. Thus this function begins with writing and ends with reading, which is not the normal way of copying things. Entering *copy_a_run*, the third argument is the address of the element that has already been read, and on exit it is the address of the first element of the next run, unless end-of-file has been reached, which is detected by a call of *feof*. Note that we inquire the value of *feof* after a read attempt, not before it, as in Pascal. Thus in C we call *fread* even if we are not certain whether there are any new data available. We then test *feof* and if it is

non-zero, we know that the read attempt has failed and we do not use the value
pointed to by the first argument of *fread.*

Example 4

We shall assume that each name in the file *PEOPLE* occurs only once, and that the
file has been sorted by program *NATMSORT* of Example 3. Write a program which
looks for a given name in the file *PEOPLE.* Use *binary search,* each time dividing
the interval to be searched into two halves. If a record with the given name is found,
increase the *length* member of that record by one (which means that the person with
that name has become 1 centimetre taller). (For the binary search method, see also
Example 4 in Section 3.7.)

The important new aspect of this program is that we need both update and direct
access facilities. The function *fseek* requires the position to be expressed in bytes,
but for us it is more convenient to deal with record numbers rather than byte
numbers. This is no serious problem, since they differ exactly by a factor *size,* the
size of a record. Though actually larger, let us assume, for example, that *size* has the
value 3, and that there are four records. The situation is then as follows:

```
byte number:   0    1    2    3    4    5    6    7    8    9    10    11
               |_____|    |_____|    |_____|    |_____|
record number:      0              1              2              3
```

We can then compute the last record number *right* = 3 as follows:

fseek(fp, −size, 2);
right = ftell(fp)/size;

The code 2 denotes the end of the file, so *ftell* yields the value 12 − *size* = 9, which is
a byte number. Dividing it by *size,* we obtain the rightmost record number
right = 9/3 = 3. Here is the program:

```
/* DIRECTACCESS: The Binary Search method is applied to a file. If a person
                 with the given name is found, his or her length is
                 increased by one. The program demonstrates both direct-
                 accessing and updating a file.                          */
#include <stdio.h>
#include "PERSFILE.H"

main( )
{ FILE *fp;
  PERSON a;
  char str[NAME_LENGTH + 1];
  long left, right, middle;
  int indicator, size;
  fp = fopen("PEOPLE", "i+"); /* Implementation dependent */
  size = sizeof(PERSON);
  printf("Enter a name to be looked up: ");
  while (scanf("%s", str), str[0] != '#')
```

```
{ left = 0L;
  fseek(fp, (long) −size, 2); right = ftell(fp)/size;
  do
  { middle = left + (right − left)/2;
    /* instead of middle = (left + right)/2,
         to reduce the danger of integer overflow                    */
    fseek(fp, middle * size, 0);
    fread(&a, size, 1, fp);
    indicator = strcmp(str, a. name);
    if (indicator <= 0) right = middle − 1;
    if (indicator >= 0) left = middle + 1;
  } while (left <= right);
  if (indicator == 0)
  { printf("Found! New length = %3d\n", ++a. length);
    fseek(fp, middle * size, 0);
    fwrite(&a, size, 1, fp);
  } else printf ("Name %s not found\n", str);
  printf ("\nAnother name, or # to stop: ");
  }
  fclose(fp);
}
```

6.9 EXERCISES

6.1 Write a program which reads a text file and computes the average of the lengths of all lines of more than 20 characters, not including the newline character at the end of each line.

6.2 Write a program which copies a text file, inserting a space immediately before and after an equal sign (=) if there is a non-blank character in such positions. For example, $x=y$ is changed into $x = y$, and $u= v$ into $u = v$, with no extra space inserted between = and v.

6.3 Write a program which asks for a sequence of integers followed by #. Then another integer is read which must be looked up in the sequence. Write the integers read from the keyboard to an unformatted file, and search this file sequentially for the given integer.

6.4 Write a program which reads a text file consisting of only words separated by spaces and newline characters. Each word is a sequence of capital letters. In alphabetic order, the distinct words are to be printed, followed by the numbers of the lines where they occur. For example, the input file

> THE OLD MAN
> AND
> THE SEA

leads to the following output:

> AND   2
> MAN   1
> OLD   1
> SEA   3
> THE   1   3

6.5 Develop an inventory information system for articles in a store. Each article has an unique number, ranging from 0 to $N-1$, where, for example, $N = 25000$. We suppose that N is too large for an array in memory but small enough to create a file containing N integers. The only relevant information for each article is the number of copies that are in store. Use a file which contains only these quantities: the ith number in the file ($i = 0, 1, \ldots, N-1$) indicates how many copies of article i are in store. Write three programs: the first program *NEWSTORE* to write N zeros to the file, corresponding to an empty store; the second, called *UPDSTORE*, which asks for article numbers and (possibly negative) corresponding quantities, to be added algebraically to the number for that article in the file; and, finally, program *PRSTORE*, to print all positive quantities, preceded by the corresponding article number. For example, suppose that, immediately after the execution of *NEWSTORE*, we run the update program *UPDSTORE* with the following input data:

```
20503      12
11004     549
17001      20
20503      -4
#
```

After this, *PRSTORE* will produce the following table:

article	in store
11004	549
17001	20
20503	8

Bibliography

Ammeraal, L. (1986). *Programming Principles in Computer Graphics,* Chichester: John Wiley.

Feuer, A., and N. Gehani (eds) (1984). *Comparing and Assessing Programming Languages Ada C Pascal,* Englewood Cliffs, NJ: Prentice-Hall.

Harbison, S. P., and G. L. Steele Jr. (1984). *C A Reference Manual,* Englewood Cliffs, NJ: Prentice-Hall.

Kernighan, B. W., and D. M. Ritchie (1978). *The C Programming Language,* Englewood Cliffs, NJ: Prentice-Hall.

Tondo, C. L., and S. E. Gimpel (1985). *The C Answer Book,* Englewood Cliffs, NJ: Prentice-Hall.

Walker, A. N. (1984). *The UNIX Environment,* Chichester: John Wiley.

Index

116

DATE

PRINTED IN U.S.A.